MARY THE MOTHER OF GOD
SERMONS BY SAINT GREGORY PALAMAS

MARY THE MOTHER OF GOD
Sermons by Saint Gregory Palamas

edited by
Christopher Veniamin

MOUNT THABOR PUBLISHING
2022

First edition 2005
First Reprint edition (with minor corrections) 2022

Mount Thabor Publishing
106 Hilltop Road
Dalton, PA 18414 USA

www.mountthabor.com

Printed in the United States of America

Library of Congress Cataloging-in-Publication Data

Gregory Palamas, Saint, 1296-1359.
[Homilies. English. Selections. 2005]
Mary the Mother of God : sermons by Saint Gregory Palamas / edited by Christopher Veniamin. -- 1st ed.
    p. cm.
ISBN 978-0-9774983-0-7 (alk. paper)
1. Mary, Blessed Virgin--Saint--Sermons. 2. Orthodox Eastern Church--Sermons--Early works to 1800. 3. Sermons, Greek--Translations into English. I. Veniamin, Christopher, 1958- II. Title.
BT608.G73 2005
232.91--dc22
                                    2005936551

Front Cover: Fourteenth century icon of the Entry of the Mother of God, Holy Monastery of Chilandar, Mount Athos.

Σωφρονίῳ Ἀθωνίτῃ
(1896 – 1993)

Saint Gregory Palamas
(1296–1359)
Chapel of the Holy Unmercenary Physicians
Vatopedi Monastery, Mount Athos

Luminary of the Orthodox faith,
support of the Church and teacher,
splendour of monastics,
invincible champion of theologians,
O wonderworker Gregory,
boast of Thessalonica,
preacher of grace,
pray without ceasing
that our souls may be saved.

Dismissal Hymn (Apolytikion) of the Saint
Fourth Plagial (Tone Eight), Second Sunday in Great Lent

CONTENTS

FOREWORD

MARY THE MOTHER OF GOD is the first volume in the series *Sermons by Saint Gregory Palamas,* the purpose of which is to bring the life and teaching of this remarkable fourteenth century saint (1296–1359) to a wider readership, to all who are interested in the rich Biblical tradition of the Church Fathers.

Arranged thematically, the work in hand consists of six sermons devoted to the Mother of our Lord, including the most celebrated of all Palamas' writings, his second sermon "On the Entry of the Mother of God into the Holy of Holies", Homily 53 in the surviving corpus of sixty-three homilies. The other sermons in this edition, in liturgical sequence and with their corresponding numbering in the corpus, are on the Holy Virgin's Nativity (Homily 42), the first sermon on the Entry (Homily 52), on the Annunciation (Homily 14), on the First to See the Risen Christ (Homily 18), and on the Dormition of the *Theotokos* (Homily 37).

Saint Gregory's sermons on the Mother of God are among the profoundest and most eloquent dedications to the Virgin Mary in Christian literature. His second homily on the Presentation or Entry may be regarded as his "masterpiece", for it stands not only as his most famous writing, but arguably as the greatest homily ever written on the Mother of our Lord, God, and Saviour.

It was in 1334, while on Mount Athos, in his third year at the

hermitage of Saint Sabas, which belongs to the Great Lavra, that
Palamas experienced a vision in which he was encouraged to share
the wisdom bestowed upon him from on high. It seemed that he
was carrying a vessel overflowing with milk, which subsequently
turned into the finest of wines. The wine emitted such a strong
fragrance that it brought great joy to his soul. A youth appeared and
rebuked him for not sharing the wine with others and for allowing
it to go to waste, for this wine, as he explained, was inexhaustible.
The angel then warned Gregory, reminding him of the parable of
the talents (cf. Matt. 25:14–30). As he later related to his friend and
disciple Dorotheus,[1] Palamas understood this vision to mean that
the time would come when he would be called upon to transfer
his teaching from the simple plane of the ethical (the milk) to
the higher plane of the dogmatic word (the wine), which leads
heavenward.[2] Thus at the age of about thirty-eight Gregory began
to write his Encomium for Saint Peter the Athonite, and, at about
the same time, he also began to compose what is without doubt
the most famous of all his works, Homily 53, "On the Entry of the
Mother of God into the Holy of Holies", in which the *Theotokos* is
presented as the archetype of the hesychastic way of life, the way
of "stillness" (Gk. *hesychia, cf.* Ps. 46:10).

The teaching of Saint Gregory and his fellow Hesychasts was
based on the understanding that man, the greatest of all God's
creatures, had been called to enter into direct and unmediated
communion with God even from this present life, and become
Christlike (cf. Gen. 1:26). The chief manner by which this is
achieved is through the grace of God and *noetic* prayer, that is,
through the Prayer of the Heart, also known as the Jesus Prayer:

1. One of the Vlatte brothers (the other being Markos), who built Vlattadon
Monastery (1351–1371). Dorotheus later also served as Archbishop of Thessalonica,
from 1371 to 1379.

2. Philotheus Kokkinos, *Encomium for our father among the Saints, Gregory Palamas,
Archbishop of Thessalonica,* ed. J.-P. Migne, *Patrologia Graeca* 151:580A–581B; see
esp. crit. ed. Demetrios G. Tsames, *The Hagiological Works of Philotheus Kokkinos,
Patriarch of Constantinople,* vol. 1: *Thessalonian Saints,* Center for Byzantine Studies
(Thessalonica, 1985), §§ 36–37, pp. 467–468.

On the Nativity of the Mother of God

THE TIME IS ALWAYS RIGHT to make a beginning of a way of life that will lead to salvation. To prove this, the great Paul says, "Behold, now is the accepted time; behold, now is the day of salvation" (2 Cor. 6:2). "Let us therefore cast off the works of darkness, and let us do the works of light. Let us walk honestly as in the day" (*cf.* Rom. 13:12–13). He does not mean that one particular hour or day is the acceptable time, but the whole period after the manifestation of Our Lord and God and Saviour Jesus Christ. When the visible sun has risen upon earth it is time for men to do physical work, as David tells us: "The sun ariseth, and man goeth forth unto his work and to his labour until the evening" (Ps. 104:22–23). In the same way, since the Sun of righteousness (Mal. 4:2) appeared to us in the flesh, all the time following His appearing is appropriate for spiritual work. The same Prophet makes this point in another passage where, after saying of the Lord's Coming, "The stone which the builders refused is become the head stone of the corner" (Ps. 118:22), he adds, "This is the day which the Lord hath made; we will rejoice and be glad in it" (Ps. 118:24). In the case of the visible sun, which is interrupted by the night, he says, "Man goes forth unto his work until the evening", but as the Sun of righteousness knows no evening, and has, according to the Epistle, "no variableness neither shadow of turning" (Jas. 1:17), it offers an unbroken opportunity for spiritual labour.

If, however, it were necessary to name the most appropriate season of all, and if, just as there is a time to sow and a time to reap, a time to plant and a time to harvest, and a time for everything else (cf. Eccl. 3:1–8), you are looking for a season especially suited for beginning a good work, then it is autumn, particularly this month, which is our first month and the start of the year, when our salvation had its origin, as we celebrate today. This sacred feast and holiday that we are keeping is the first to commemorate our recall and re-creation according to grace, for on it all things began to be made new, enduring precepts began to be brought in instead of temporary ones, the spirit instead of the letter, the truth instead of shadows.

Today a new world and a mysterious paradise have been revealed, in which and from which a New Adam came into being, re-making the Old Adam and renewing the universe. He is not led astray by the deceiver, but deceives him, and bestows freedom on those enslaved to sin through his treachery. Today a paradoxical book has been made ready on earth, which in an indescribable way can hold, not the imprint of words, but the living Word Himself; not a word consisting of air, but the heavenly Word; not a word that perishes as soon as it is formed, but the Word Who snatches those who draw near Him from perdition; not a word made by the movement of a man's tongue, but the Word begotten of God the Father before all ages. Today the living Tabernacle of God not made with hands appears, the inspired human Ark of the true Bread of Life sent down from heaven for us (cf. John 6:32ff). Today, according to the Psalms, "Truth has sprung up from the earth", the true image of human nobility which comes from above, "and righteousness has looked down from heaven" (Ps. 85:11 Lxx). This righteousness has deposed the unrighteous ruler from his unjust dominion, after being wrongfully condemned by him and rightly condemning him, and having bound the strong and evil one, plundered his goods (cf. Matt. 12:29), and transformed them, rendering them receptive to divine righteousness. Thus Christ took sin's prisoners to live with Him for ever, justifying them by faith in Him, but He bound the prince of sin with inescapable bonds, and delivered him to eternal fire without light. Today, as prophesied, out of the "stem of Jesse" a rod has come forth (*cf.* Isa. 11:1), from which a flower has grown which knows no wilting. This rod recalls our human nature, which had withered and fallen away from the unfading garden of delight, makes it bloom again, grants it to flourish for ever, brings it up to heaven, and leads it into paradise. With this rod the great Shepherd moves His human flock to eternal pastures, and supported by this rod, our nature lays aside its old age and feeble senility, and easily strides towards heaven, leaving the earth below for those who, devoid of support, are plunging downwards.

But who is the new world, the mysterious paradise, the paradoxical book, the inspired Tabernacle and Ark of God, the truth sprung from the earth, the much-extolled rod of Jesse? It is the Maiden who before and after childbearing is eternally virgin, whose birth from a barren mother we celebrate today. Joachim and Anna lived together blamelessly before God, but seemed to the Israelites to be at fault according to the Law because they remained childless. Since there was not yet any hope of immortality, the continuance of the race was seen as an absolute necessity. Now that this Virgin born today has bestowed eternity upon us by bearing a child in virginity, having children to succeed us is no longer necessary, but in those days having many children was regarded as superior to virtue, and childlessness was such a great evil, that these just people were rebuked for their lack of children, rather than praised for their virtue. Deeply saddened by these reproaches, the righteous couple called to mind Abraham and Sarah, and the others who had suffered grief because of their childlessness. They then considered the healing remedy for that sorrow, which some had found, and decided that they too would resort to beseeching God. The chaste Joachim departed to the wilderness and dwelt there, fasting and offering up prayer to God that he might become a father. And before he ceased praying or returned thence, he received full assurance that his request would be granted. Meanwhile, the like-minded Anna shut herself in a nearby garden and cried to the Lord with pain in her heart, "Hear me, O God of my fathers, and bless me, as you blessed Sarah's womb." And the Lord heard them and blessed them, and promised to give them a child. Now He has fulfilled this promise and has granted them a daughter more wonderful than all the wonders down through the ages, the Mother of the Creator of the universe, who made the human race divine, turned earth into heaven, made God into the Son of man, and men into the sons of God. For she conceived within herself without seed, and brought forth in a way past telling, the One Who brought everything that exists out of non-being, and transformed it into something good, Who will never let it cease to exist.

Why did she come from a barren womb? In order to put an end to her parents' sorrow, transform their disgrace, and prefigure that deliverance from the grief and curse of the Forefathers of the human race, which was to come about through her. She alone dwelt in the Holy of Holies, and she alone became the abode of the Creator of the natural order, so how could nature dare profane the womb in which she rested, and from which she came forth? Neither before nor after her had there appeared a virgin mother or a mother of God, and no one before or after her had dwelt in the Holy of Holies, so it was fitting that no other infant was seen to have been conceived within her mother's womb before or afterwards. As the Mother of God had to be a virgin of David's stock, born at the right moment for our salvation, the time drew near and the Virgin had to be made ready, but even among David's descendants no others were found at that time superior in virtue or in nobility of character and birth to that childless couple. So those without children were preferred to those with many, that the Daughter with all virtues might be born of highly virtuous parents, the All-pure of those who were exceptionally chaste, and that chastity, conceiving through prayer and asceticism, might as a consequence become the mother of virginity, virginity which would bring forth without corruption the divinity begotten of the virgin Father before all ages. What wings that prayer had! How boldly it approached God! How spotlessly pure their hearts must have been to offer a prayer which so speedily achieved so much! A miracle was needed to prepare the way for the great wonder, and nature had gradually to give way to grace.

But you, O sacred audience, who listen to my words, my human flock and field in Christ, offer your exercise of the virtues and your progress in them as a birthday gift to the Mother of God: both men and women, elderly people along with younger ones, rich and poor, leaders and subjects, those of absolutely every race, age, rank, profession and branch of learning. Let none of you have a soul which is barren and without fruit. Let nobody be unloving or unreceptive to the spiritual seed. May each of you eagerly accept this celestial seed, the word of salvation (cf. Luke 8:11), and by your own efforts bring it to perfection as a heavenly work and fruit pleasing to God. Let no one make a beginning of a good work which brings no fruit to perfection (cf. Luke 8:14), nor declare his faith in Christ only with his tongue. "Not every one", it says, "that saith unto me, Lord, Lord, shall enter into the kingdom of heaven, but he that doeth the will of my Father which is in heaven" (Matt. 7:21), and, "No man, having put his hand to the plough, and looking back, is fit for the kingdom of God" (Luke 9:62).

Virgins who are vowed to the monastic life, and those of you who have done well and returned to live in a community of virgins after being married, and all of you in general who have chosen to live together in this way out of a desire to repent: live according to God in all things on account of the Virgin born on this day for our sake, who as a virgin gave birth according to the flesh to Him Who was begotten of the virgin Father before eternity. Live for her and the only God, Who was incarnate of her, looking only to Him, making Him your sole delight, rejoicing in hope, patient in tribulation (Rom. 12:12), obedient to those in authority over you, serving one another, striving for peace one with another, waiting constantly with attention and prayer and contrition of soul, with both psalms and hymns, and spiritual songs (Eph. 5:19). Be pure and unsullied in body and soul, in all your senses and your understanding, and show forth in all respects your spiritual and virginal way of life. Thus, according to the Psalm, you shall follow behind the Mother of God, and be brought as her companions (*cf.* Ps. 45:14), and enter the temple not made with hands of the King of Heaven, into the heavenly and eternal bridechamber of incorruption.

Those of you who are married should not surrender yourselves entirely to this world. For the Mother of God, this newly established world higher than the world, appeared today as the fruit of married life. You who are old, demonstrate that your thinking is worthy of old age, and do not imitate youth's rashness in your words, thoughts and actions to your own detriment, being carnally minded and living according to the flesh. Young people, emulate the elderly, respect them and obey them. Do not be ignorant of how honourable old age is, or that youth is not inferior to august old age. If you are unaware of this, ask the wise Solomon and you will hear, "If men have understanding, they have grey hairs enough, and an unspotted life is the true ripeness of old age" (Wisd. 4:9). Those of you who possess an abundance of the unstable goods of this world, which slip away and often pass from one person to another, will, by giving them away, trade them for eternal life for yourselves. "For a man's life consisteth not in the abundance of the things which he possesseth" (Luke 12:15). As for those of you who lack necessities, be rich in patience and thanksgiving to God, that you may be numbered with those poor whom He pronounces blessed, and inherit the kingdom of heaven (Matt. 5:3; Luke 6:20). Rulers, "execute true judgment" (Zech. 7:9), and do not use force against those in your power, which is unjust, but show a fatherly disposition towards them, bearing in mind that you are of the same race as they and a fellow-servant. Nor should you be unjustifiably vexed on account of submission to the Church and its teaching, for these things are a sure proof of men of good will. Subjects, you ought only to obey your rulers in matters which do not deprive you of our promised hope of the kingdom of heaven (*cf.* Matt. 22:21).

Offer now with one accord to the Virgin, whose feast we keep today, the most desirable and appropriate gift, your sanctification and bodily purity through self-control and prayer. See, all of you, how chastity, fasting and prayer, linked with contrition, made Joachim and Anna the parents of a divine vessel, a vessel chosen not just to bear the name of God, like Paul (Acts 9:15) who was to be born later, but to bear Him "Whose name is Wonderful" (*cf.* Isa. 9:6; Ps. 8:1 Lxx). If we persevere in our prayers, as well as the other virtues, continuing in God's temple with understanding, we shall find stored up within ourselves that purity of heart, which holds God and manifests Him to us. It is this purity, and the soul's corresponding disposition towards God, that Isaiah calls the spirit of salvation within the womb, saying to the Lord, "On account of thy fear, O Lord, we have been with child, we have been in travail, we have conceived the spirit of thy salvation which we have wrought upon earth" (Isa. 26:18 Lxx). Do you see how barren, fruitless souls bear fine children? However, after the words we have quoted the Prophet adds, "We shall not fall, but the inhabitants of the earth shall fall", meaning those who wallow in earthly thoughts and passions.

If we too, brethren, wish to dwell not on earth but in heaven, and not to fall to the ground or into sin that pulls us down, but to reach out continuously towards the divine heights, let us fear God, abstain from everything evil, return to Him through good works, and strive by self-control and prayer to wipe out the evil accretions within us, to change our inner thoughts for the better, and, according to the Prophet, to be in labour with the spirit of salvation and bring it to birth, having as our helper, through invoking her name, the Virgin who was today bestowed upon her parents through prayer and a manner of life pleasing to God. She transformed their sorrow, annulled the ancestral curse, and brought our first Mother's pangs to an end, painlessly bearing Christ as a virgin.

To Whom belong all glory, honour and worship together with His Father without beginning and the all-holy, good and life-giving Spirit, now and for ever and unto the ages of ages. Amen.

On the Entry of the Mother of God into the Holy of Holies I

I F A TREE IS KNOWN BY ITS FRUIT, and a good tree brings forth good fruit (*cf.* Matt. 7:17; Luke 6:43–44), how could she who is the Mother of Goodness, who gave birth to that Beauty which has no beginning, not be incomparably more excellent and beautiful than anything good on earth and in heaven? The Power Who made all things fair, the co-sempeternal, express Image of Goodness, the pre-eternal, sublime and most excellent Word of the heavenly Father, wished in His ineffable love and compassion for mankind to put on our image in order to recall our human nature, which had been dragged down into the inmost recesses of Hades, to renew it after it had grown old, and to raise it up to the heavenly heights of His kingdom and divinity. He united His Person with our humanity, and, since it was necessary for Him to assume flesh that was both new and our own, in order to renew us by means of what was ours, He also had to be carried in the womb and brought forth as we are, then nurtured after birth and brought up as was appropriate. Becoming like us in all respects for our sake, He found the Ever-Virgin, whom we extol and whose mysterious Entry into the Holy of Holies we celebrate today, to be a most suitable handmaid in every way, able to bestow on Him an undefiled nature from her own. God determined before all ages that she should be for the salvation and restoration of our race, and chose her from all mankind down through the ages, not simply from among ordinary people, but from all the elect of every age who were admired and renowned for their piety, their understanding, and their ways, words and deeds which were beneficial to all as well as pleasing to God.

In the beginning the supremely evil spiritual Serpent rose up against us and drew us down to the depths of Hades. There were many factors which stirred him up against us, and by means of which he enslaved human nature: envy, jealousy, hatred, injustice, deceit, false reasoning and, in addition to such evils, that deadly power he possessed, which he had engendered in himself as the first to depart from true Life. He envied Adam from the start when he saw him dwelling in the garden of incorruptible delight, surrounded by the radiance of godlike glory, and being led up from earth to heaven, whence he, the devil, had been justly cast down. In his envy he raged against man with the utmost fury, to the point of wanting to put him to death. Jealousy is the father not only of hatred but also of murder, which the deceitful snake, the hater of mankind, inflicted on us linked with guile. Completely unjustly he desired absolute power over man, so as to ruin the creature formed by God in His own image and likeness. Since, however, he did not dare to attack man to his face, he used treachery and cunning. By means of the visible snake, the terrible enemy and traitor approached as a friend and good counsellor, and, without being detected, managed to pour the deadly venom of his power into man by giving him advice against God.

If Adam had held fast then to the divine commandment and rejected the evil counsel to go against it, he would have been shown to be victorious over his opponent and superior to deadly corruption, by forcefully putting his frenzied and treacherous assailant to shame. Because, however, he willingly gave in, as he ought on no account to have done, he suffered defeat and came to nothing. As the root of the human race, he produced us as shoots subject to death just as he was. If we were to struggle to overcome our defeat, regain victory, shake off the venom killing our souls and bodies and lay hold once more on eternal life free from harm, our human race obviously needed a new root, a New Adam, who was not only sinless, but also completely incapable of being deceived or defeated. He also had to be able to forgive sins, to make the guilty innocent, and not just to live but to bring others to life, so that he could pass on life and remission of sins to those who attached themselves to him and belonged to the same stock, and restore to life not just those who died from then on, but also those who had died before his time.

Paul, the great trumpet of the Spirit, cried out saying, "The first man was made a living soul; the second man was made a quickening spirit" (cf. 1 Cor. 15:45, 47; Gen. 2:7). No one but God is sinless, life-creating and able to forgive sins. So the New Adam had to be not only a man but God: to be, literally, Life, Wisdom, Righteousness, Mercy and everything else good, in order to accomplish the renewal of the Old Adam and his restoration to life with mercy, wisdom and justice: the very opposite of those evil means used by the spiritual and most wicked Serpent to cause us to grow old and die.

Whereas he who was a murderer from the beginning (John 8:44) rose up against us out of jealousy and hatred, the Prince of Life (Acts 3:15) was moved to act for our sake because of His surpassing love for man and His goodness. He truly desired the salvation of His creature by bringing him once more under His authority and rescuing him, just as the originator of evil unjustly longed to destroy the work of God's hands by bringing man into subjection to himself and imposing his absolute authority. The enemy achieved his victory and man's fall by means of injustice, guile, deceit and false reasoning, but the Liberator brought about the final defeat of the chief of evil and the renewal of His creature by means of righteousness, wisdom and truth. But now is not the time to speak of the wisdom revealed in the divine dispensation.

Precise justice demanded that the same human nature which had been willingly enslaved and defeated must fight to win back victory and rid itself of voluntary servitude. For that reason it was God's good pleasure to assume our nature from us, uniting it mysteriously with His Person. His sublime purity beyond our understanding could not, however, become one with defiled human nature. Only this is impossible for God: to be joined in union with something impure before it has been cleansed. A completely undefiled and most pure virgin was needed to carry in her womb and give birth to the Lover and Giver of purity. This virgin was marked out beforehand, brought to perfection and revealed, and the mystery concerning her was fulfilled, by many wonderful happenings from various times in the past converging into one.

Those other wonders which at some time contributed to this great mystery are also celebrated by us today, because we recognize from the outcome just how significant those events were which led to so great an end. He Who is from God, with God and is God, the Word and Son of God Who, like the heavenly Father, has no beginning and no end, becomes the Son of man, the Son of the Ever-Virgin. "Jesus Christ the same yesterday, and today, and for ever" (Heb. 13:8), unchanging in His divinity, blameless in His humanity. He alone, as Isaiah had already foretold, "did no sin, neither was guile found in his mouth" (1 Pet. 2:22; *cf.* Isa. 53:9). Moreover, He alone was not shapen in iniquity and conceived in sin (*cf.* Ps. 51:5), as David testified concerning himself and everyone else, in order that He might also be completely pure and undefiled in respect of the flesh He had assumed, and would not require any purifying sacrifices for Himself on its account. Thus He could accept purification, the Passion, Death and Resurrection for our sake, transferring them to us, with profound justice and wisdom. For the physical impulse to reproduce is involuntary and does not obey the law of our mind, although some people do bring it forcibly into subjection, and others chastely give rein to it solely for the purpose of begetting children. It brings with it the signs of original condemnation, being synonymous with corruption and producing children who will obviously perish, and it is the passionate urge of human beings who did not retain the dignity assigned to our nature by God, but have become like beasts.

God was not just born among men, but born of a holy and pure virgin or, more precisely, of this exceedingly pure and most holy of virgins who was not only above any physical stain, but also far beyond the reach of any defiled, carnal thoughts. Her conception of Christ resulted from the all-holy Spirit coming upon her, not from fleshly desire, and was preceded by the annunciation and her faith in the in-dwelling of God in a manner we cannot describe, as it was outside the normal course of events and beyond words, but not by submission to, or any experience of, passionate desire. Having utterly banished such desire by prayer and spiritual joy, she conceived and gave birth – "Behold the handmaid of the Lord; be it unto me according to thy word" (Luke 1:38). In order that there would be a virgin equal to this task, God pre-ordained this ever-virgin Maid whom we extol today, and chose her from among His elect down through the ages.

Note the starting-point of God's election. The excellent Seth was chosen by God from among Adam's children (cf. Gen. 4:25-5:8). By his orderly conduct, his control over his senses and his magnificent virtue he showed himself to be a living heaven, and so he became one of God's chosen (Luke 3:38), from whom the Virgin would appear as a chariot fit to bear God Who transcends the heavens, to call men back to adoption as sons of the heavenly Father.

That is why all Seth's descendants were called God's sons (Gen. 6:2, 4), because from this race the Son of God was to be born the Son of man. The name Seth can be interpreted to mean "resurrection", or, "a rising up from", which actually refers to the Lord, Who promises and gives everlasting life to those who believe in Him. How appropriate a figure Seth was to represent Christ! Seth was born to Eve, as Eve herself says, "instead of Abel" (Gen. 4:25), whom Cain envied and murdered, whereas the Virgin's Son, Christ, came to the human race instead of Adam, whom the prince and patron of evil killed out of envy. Seth, however, did not raise up Abel, as he merely foreshadowed the Resurrection, but Our Lord Jesus Christ resurrected Adam. He is the true Life and Resurrection of mankind, through Whom Seth's descendants were deemed worthy, in hope, of divine adoption, being called sons of God (*cf.* Gen. 6:2–4). That they were referred to as God's sons on account of this hope, is demonstrated by the first man to be so called and to attain God's election. This was Seth's son Enos who, as Moses wrote, "was the first who hoped to be called by God's name" (Gen. 4:26 Lxx). Do you see that it was through hope that he came to be called after God?

Having begun with Adam's sons, God's selection, according to His foreknowledge, for the sake of the future Mother of God, was accomplished down through the generations until it reached the King and Prophet David, the successors to his throne and his descendants. When the time came for God's choice to reach its culmination, Joachim and Anna, of the house and lineage of David, were picked out by Him. They were childless, but lived chastely together and were more virtuous than all those who traced back their noble descent and character to David. With asceticism and prayer they begged God to deliver them from childlessness, and promised to dedicate to Him from infancy the child to be born to them. She who is now the Mother of God was promised and given to them by God as their daughter, that the girl with every virtue might be born of virtuous parents, the all-pure Maid of those who were exceptionally chaste, and that chastity, coming together with prayer and asceticism, might become as a result the mother of virginity, that virginity which in purity brought forth, according to the flesh, Him Who was begotten before all ages in respect of His divinity, of a virgin Father. O, the wings of that prayer! With what boldness it came before God!

Since they had obtained that for which they had prayed, and knew the divine promise to them had been fulfilled, they in turn kept their promise to God. Being truthful people, dear to God and God-loving, they hastened, as soon as she was weaned, to bring the most holy Virgin, God's child and now the Mother of God, to His Temple, to the Chief Priest there. Even at that tender age, being full of divine graces and not wanting in the perfection of her mental faculties, she understood, more than anyone else did at the time, what was happening to her. She showed as best she could that, rather than being led, she was coming to God by herself and of her own volition, as though it were natural for her to fly towards holy and divine love, and to consider entering the Holy of Holies and dwelling there as something desirable which she knew was fitting for her.

When God's High Priest understood that the Maid apparently possessed divine grace above all others, he had to count her worthy of something more excellent than anyone else deserved. He led her into the Holy of Holies and then persuaded everyone to be content with what had happened. At the same time, God was also helping, showing His approval and sending heavenly nourishment defying description to the Virgin in that place, by the hand of an angel. This food strengthened her physically, and she was sustained and perfected in body with more purity and excellence than the bodiless angels, having heavenly beings to minister to her. She was not simply brought once into the Holy of Holies but was, as it were, taken into God's company for a period of several years, so that through her, when the time came, the heavenly mansions might be opened and be given as everlasting dwellings to those who believe in her mysterious childbearing.

In this way, and for these reasons, she who was chosen from the elect of all ages, who was declared the holy of holies, whose body was purer and more divine than spirits cleansed by virtue, to such an extent that she was able to receive not just the form of divine words but the Person of the only-begotten Word of the Father without beginning, was today justly consigned to the innermost hallowed sanctuary like God's treasure. When the time came, this treasure was to be used to enrich and adorn both heaven and earth, as indeed came to pass. Thus and on this account the Lord glorified His Mother before she gave birth as well as afterwards. As for us, understanding the salvation which was begun for us through her, may we render as much thanksgiving and praise as we can. In the Gospel it is written that a woman, having listened for a while to the Lord's saving words, gratefully pronounced a blessing on His Mother and gave thanks, lifting up her voice and crying out to the Lord from the crowd, "Blessed is the womb that bare thee, and the paps which thou hast sucked" (Luke 11:27). As for us, we constantly have the words of eternal life in writing, and not just Christ's sayings but also His miracles, His Sufferings, and the raising up of our human nature from the dead, accomplished by these Sufferings, its ascension from earth to heaven and the everlasting life and irrevocable salvation promised to us as a result. So how can we do other than extol and bless without ceasing the Mother of the Bestower of salvation, the Giver of life, celebrating her conception, her birth, and now her coming to dwell in the Holy of Holies?

Let us too, brethren, move our dwelling-place from earth to on high. Let us be changed from flesh to spirit, and transfer our longing from fleeting concerns to things that endure. Let us despise the pleasures of the flesh, which were invented as a bait to trap the soul, and soon pass away, and let us desire spiritual gifts which stay incorruptible. Let us raise our disposition and our thoughts from the disorder below and lift them up to the heavenly sanctuary, to that Holy of Holies where the Mother of God now dwells.

So shall our songs and prayers to her come before her with boldness pleasing to God for our benefit. Then, by her intercession, we shall be heirs not only of good things here and now, but of those lasting blessings to come, by the grace and love for mankind of Him Who was born of her for our sake, Jesus Christ Our Lord, to Whom belong glory, honour and worship, together with the Father Who is without beginning and the co-eternal, life-giving Spirit, now and for ever and unto the ages of ages. Amen.

ON THE ENTRY OF THE MOTHER OF GOD INTO THE HOLY OF HOLIES II

WHEN TASKS EXCEED HUMAN STRENGTH, whether it be necessary to move something very heavy or to engage in a struggle with words, men outstanding in their excellent physical strength and eloquence find themselves in the same position as those completely incapable in both respects, because they are all equally unable to achieve anything or to succeed in their purpose. If someone attempts to touch the stars with his hand, even though he is tall and stretches his arm further than the rest, he is almost as far away from those ethereal heights as men of much shorter stature, the difference not being worth mentioning. In the same way, on subjects transcending words, eminent speakers are not significantly better at saying something than anyone else. Who can attempt to treat of matters which utterly defy all words without being seen to give way beneath the weight of these topics, like those reputed to have boasted they could counterbalance the weight of the universe, or those in the myth who attempted to make their way up to heaven? Men who make such attempts are as far from the truth as their aims are beyond the grasp of human minds and speech, being outside the sphere of this world, based far above the earth and its surroundings, and reckoned among things holy and divine.

The highest summit of all the saints, the Mother of God, passes, in the words of the Psalm, "Into the place of the wonderful tabernacle", entering the Holy of Holies "with the voice of joy and praise" (Ps. 42:4 Lxx), the inspired sound of those escorting her then, and us keeping the festival now. She is more exalted than the saints in heaven, and not only would it be impossible for anyone on his own to come anywhere near to honouring her as she deserves, but neither could all those together who have been saved by her Son, even if all were to be united as one voice. The whole creation would fall short of offering her the glory that befits her, for she has become the mother of the Creator of all. How could any words of ours adequately express the great things done for her by her Son, even taking all of us together? Would our words not be as the tiniest drop of water compared with the inexpressible abyss of her glory? Thus is this undertaking beyond my powers, and so far am I from supposing that I can devise words of praise commensurate with the superhuman virtue of the Mother of God, she who is truly blessed and superior in every way to the entire creation.

But how else can I fulfil my longing, settle my debt, or express my thanks for her countless gracious gifts to me, except by extolling her as best I can? For love persuades me and obligation, both our common indebtedness and my own personal duty, compels me. The grace which I have already received promises forgiveness hereafter for what follows, and the unfailing love for mankind of the ever-virgin Bride is a continual presence among all those who hear, encompassing all things and holding them in being. For she is near and ever standing by those who call upon her, through her tireless and most effective intercession to God her Son, which accomplishes all things for our good, as we ourselves know, having learnt from the benefits we have received, and having had our faith strengthened as a result.

Calling upon her with this faith, I hope to have her as my support to the end as I plunge now into the ocean of her wonders. I do not consider it necessary to make excuses to you who are around me for what will come later in my homily. You will easily forgive when you take everything into account: the speaker, the words, the extraordinary subject, and also the fact that each of you also needs everyone else's forgiveness when you compose various hymns to the Mother of God. (And, of course, many such hymns are written by you, because we are all obliged to pay this tribute to the Mother of God, as a community and as individuals, alone and in co-operation with others.) But even as you attempt to render the praise you owe, still you realize that you are far from extolling her as is meet. For that reason you also share the odes composed for her down through the ages, and continually, every day and hour, form an inspired, harmonious and ceaseless choir around the heavenly bridechamber.

Come then, holy company, hallowed audience, choir in harmony with the Holy Spirit, and assist me with this address, making it a joint effort, not just by listening attentively and directing your thoughts, but also by providing help through your sincere prayers, that the Word of the Father may join in from heaven with my words about His Mother, and grant that I may not strike a completely discordant note, but rather produce something pleasing to the ears of God-loving men. Those who prepare themselves for such feats need God's abundant aid, for they are accomplished only by heavenly inspiration, and are more fitting and perfect than anything else achieved down the ages. In the beginning, God put on earth every kind of sensible, sentient creature, but as none of these at all had a mind, He formed man with this capacity. As the human race progressed, there was no one able to contain God, as the situation demanded, "By whom are all things, and for whom are all things", to use the apostle's phrase (cf. Heb. 2:10). So later He graciously willed to create this ever-virgin Maid, His palace, if I may use the expression, who was shown to be capable of holding the fullness of the Godhead bodily (Col. 2:9) on account of her utmost purity, able not simply to contain Him but – O marvellous wonder! – to bring Him to birth and to form for all men, before and after her time, ties of kinship with God.

Two races were chosen by God throughout the ages, and between these two stands the Mother of God, conspicuous in her pre-eminence, the living image of everything good, the human icon of every virtue, the shrine and focal point of divine and human graces, to be emulated, as it were, by heaven and earth and what lies beyond them, to the common benefit of all. She is the sacred starting point of the spiritual Israel, by which I mean all Christian people, because she was the cause of Him who is above all causality, and through Him she lifted men up from the earth and rendered them heavenly, showing them to be spirit instead of flesh, and making them children of God. As for the carnal Israel, of whom she was born according to the flesh, she exalted her ancestors to such glory that through her they are called God's forefathers. Indeed, to express the honour of the virgin Bride as is her due, she did not just act as a mediator for certain chosen races, but, standing between God and every race of men, she made God the Son of man, and men the sons of God. She alone was shown to be the natural mother of God in a supernatural way, and by her indescribable child-bearing she became the Queen of the entire creation in this world and beyond, for "all things were made by him" who was born of her, "and without him was not any thing made that was made" (John 1:3).

The symbols of her rule are not that she has at her disposal crowns such as the masses will never touch, nor choice gems, ornaments and fabrics, nor regal costume different from the attire of common people. Such things were invented for those kings who cannot rise above what is earthly, and whose clothes reign rather than their souls. Instead, the tokens of her royal power are indescribable graces beyond our comprehension, abilities and energies surpassing nature and directed heavenwards, higher still than the adornments of heaven. They are prophecies and divine tidings transforming the laws of nature for the better; the coming of the divine Spirit, the overshadowing by the power of the Highest, the extraordinary combination of conception and virginity; the self-emptying of God's Word; the pregnancy of the ever-virgin Maid; and most miraculous of miracles: the delivery of a babe from the womb, the birth from a mother who knew no husband, without destroying the symbols of virginity, but preserving them intact.

Who can look into the innermost sanctuary, not to mention enter its depths? Who can reach even the outer doors of the place where He who dwells far above all that exists rested, the King of heaven and sovereign Lord, who by His nature has power over all things? What words can come anywhere near being worthy of her, even if, without attempting to speak of her directly, they tell of matters concerning her, which happened before and after her indescribable child-bearing? Who can adequately describe how she was provided with ineffable nourishment, how people were guided from above to come from far away to venerate her, the praise sung by a multitude of angels which united heaven and earth, and brought both into obedience to this universal Queen? Prior to all these events, however, and because of them, there were pronouncements by inspired prophets, miracles which obscurely foreshadowed the great miracle to come, spiritual ordinances which prefigured in various ways the truth that was to be, changes affecting nations and history which opened the way for the new mystery to be accomplished, the promise which God made and kept to Joachim and Anna that they would have a child in old age, although they had been childless since their youth, and this admirable couple's vow to God that they would give back the gift of their daughter to the giver. In accordance with this truly worthy and most righteous vow, they went up to the holy Temple with their promised child, and the heavenly Queen made her extraordinary entry into the Holy of Holies, the place reserved solely for God, where He once a year received the current high priests when they went in (Exod. 30:10, Lev. 16:2, 34, Heb. 9:7), and where the Virgin Mother entered at three years of age, and stayed for our sake.

We keep festival this day because we have seen the prize won for the good of us all by her unrivalled patient endurance there: God's marvellous descent to earth through her and our own glorious ascent to heaven through Him. While the holy Maid dwelt in the innermost sanctuary, she "Made high ascents in her heart" (Ps. 84:5 Lxx), which truly reached as far as the heavens themselves, and drew the heavenly Lord thence to us. There, according to the Scripture, "The king's daughter was all glorious within" (Ps. 45:13), and, as she was vastly superior to the rest of mankind in the inexpressible beauty of her purity, it pleased the Creator to prepare from her, His creature, as from radiant gold, an image sharing His divine nature, and "being made in the likeness of men" (Phil. 2:7) – O Lord, how ineffable is your love for mankind! – He adapted the work of His hands to be worthy of Him, its Maker.

Do you see how the Virgin's wreath was woven? Do you see how we all benefit from her royal attire? How it was not by chance that the virgin Queen of all brought her fellow human beings into subjection to herself and ruled over them. She attributed nothing more than names to herself, and brought her compatriots into submission in accordance with earthly ordinances, which permit some people to rise higher than those prostrate, but not than those standing upright. But she exalted all those below her through herself, and showed what it meant to be a heavenly subject instead of an earthly one. Partaking of higher honour, superior power and heavenly election, she became the highest Queen of all and the most blessed Sovereign of a blessed race, sending out all around her, from both body and soul, bright and holy rays of light. Wishing to establish an icon of everything good, and to give a clear demonstration to both angels and men that He was able to do so, the Creator made her an adornment of things visible and invisible. He brought together a blend of all divine and human graces, a sublime beauty to enhance both worlds. Thus He truly made her of such exquisite beauty, uniting all the separate components with which He had adorned the universe, showing us an extraordinary aspect of that creative power which is exclusively His, as was truly fitting for the Mother of the light.

In the beginning, when God set the greater light to rule the day, first He made light scattered freely everywhere, then the disc of the sun to receive it (Gen. 1:1–3, 16–18). In the same way, He now displayed His ever-virgin Mother as the lampstand of the divine, ineffable light of everything virtuous. Whereas previously goodness had been dispersed among all, later every kind of virtue was brought together in her in a way past understanding or description, so high had she ascended. All those things which, distributed to the noblest of every age, were sufficient to make them great, and everything which those angels and men who found favour with God were in part, she gathered together. She alone, having brought all these gifts to perfection and multiplied them inexpressibly, pours out abundant grace on those who honour her, also granting that they may reach up to her as the receptacle of great graces, and in her goodness lavishing even more excellent favours upon them. Nor will she ever cease being mercifully disposed towards all mankind, providing everything beneficial and assisting us plentifully.

Anybody who considers how she represents and bestows everything good, will say that the Virgin fulfils the same rôle as regards virtue for those living virtuously as the sun does in relation to visible light for those who live by it, and that what happened to light in the beginning foreshadowed and prefigured the wonders to be accomplished later concerning her. If, however, you turn the eyes of your understanding towards the Sun, who rose marvellously upon men from her, and who has by His nature all the gifts which accrued to her by grace, and more besides; if you turn your mind's eye to Him, the Virgin will immediately appear to be heaven, blessed with the possession of everything noble, and as much more radiant than divinely favoured beings both on earth and in heaven, just as the heavens are larger than the sun, though the sun is brighter than the heavens.

What words, O Mother of God and Virgin, can describe your divinely radiant beauty? Your qualities cannot be circumscribed by thoughts or words, for they transcend our minds and speech. But it is possible to sing your praises if you, in your charity, so permit. In you all graces are to be found. You are the perfection of nobleness in all its forms, the living portrait of every virtue and kindness. You alone were vouchsafed the gifts of the Spirit in their totality, or rather, you alone held mysteriously in your womb Him in whom are the treasures of all these spiritual gifts, and became inexplicably His tabernacle. Therefore, you were the object of His care from your infancy, even in respect of physical needs, and He paradoxically accepted you from your childhood as His companion, showing from that time forward, by means of such strange events as this, that you were the unchanging shrine of all His graces.

You were deemed worthy of much higher privileges than were granted to other men. Your birth was extraordinary, your upbringing even stranger, and your childbearing, without knowing anything of men, was yet more supremely mysterious. Whereas your birth was adorned with pledges made by God and human beings, that is to say, by your parents – for when they received His promise they rightly vowed you, the promised child, to Him in return – you yourself were also beautified with heavenly promises at various times, and enriched the whole world with them. Before long you received the tidings of Him from whom and through whom so great a promise was made (Luke 1:26–38), that the promises to God's friends down through the ages which found fulfilment in you, and the great visions they beheld, seemed merely like obscure reflections and vague ideas in comparison. You alone fulfilled all their visions, surpassing our common human nature by means of your union with God, not just when you gave birth in a marvellous way, but also through the preceding fellowship with Him in everything good, which resulted from your utter purity.

It was fitting that the Mother of Him who is "fairer than the sons of men" (Ps. 45:2) should herself be altogether unrivalled and be furnished by her child with amazing beauty, in order that, completely resembling her in every detail, He might be recognized as the Son of the ever-virgin Maid, because of His obvious likeness to her in all respects. Thus, everyone whose eyes beheld Him would proclaim the origin according to the flesh of the Son without human father. It would clearly have been unreasonable if He, who by His word formed this universe and made it fair with all sorts of beautiful things, had not passed on to her that same power to create beauty, which through her He Himself was to receive by nature, and in which He knew that shortly He was to share. This is why He who adorned the lilies of the field more excellently than Solomon's royal attire (Matt. 6:28–29, Luke 12:27), also arrayed the Virgin, from whom He would be clothed in human flesh, in this extraordinary fashion, making her admirable in the eyes of all, as she is the divine repository of every single noble and good attribute, and of them all collectively. In her alone, of all men down through the ages, there is absolutely no sign of any deficiency in any respect. She is as far superior to all in everything as the heavens are higher than the earth, to such an extent that she appears to us as though to men standing at a great distance, like star-gazers, looking steadfastly in her direction.

The reason mankind was brought into being by God was so that they might apprehend with their senses the sky, the earth, and everything they contain, as visible objects, and by means of them go beyond them with their minds to invisible beauties, that they might sing the praises of God, the one Creator of all. No one could say, however, that the Virgin whom we now extol was made for this purpose, but rather in order to persuade those who beheld her to marvel at the Creator. She appeared on earth in all her manifold beauty, as a great wonder outshining heavenly luminaries and angels. It had to be so, because if "the king's daughter is all glorious from within" (Ps. 45:13 Lxx), her outward appearance and everything about her could not be out of keeping, but were rightly in harmony and concord with what lay within.

This will become clear to you when you realize that the psalmist-prophet's thoughts are tending in the same direction. For he does not say that all the glory of the king's daughter is "within", but "from within" (Ps. 45:13 Lxx), meaning that it pours forth like light from within her to without, revealing to all those who see it the magnificence stored up inside her on account of her complete freedom from passion, and making known the exquisite beauty of her virginal soul. If the chaste Joseph is rightly called "all-beautiful" (cf. Gen. 39:6), the all-pure Virgin is surely worthiest of all to be so addressed. Is she not as superior to him in beauty as virginity is to chastity, especially virginity which is a match for the angels? Or rather, does she not surpass him to the same extent as all virtue and grace, dwelling together with purest virginity in a single soul, surpass chastity? It might not be appropriate to call Joseph all-beautiful in every respect, or perhaps he is called all-beautiful only with regard to his body. By contrast, however, even the Virgin's soul is synonymous with everything good, which she bears as truly all-beautiful in her most pure body, so that to those who see as we do, it appears to come from without, but to the discerning spirit of prophecy it is known to come from within.

Possessing so many spiritual gifts and natural endowments from her mother's womb, she did not take in any sort of additional knowledge – for this in my opinion is how we should regard what is learned from lessons – by studying with teachers. Instead, making her sovereign mind obedient to God in everything, she decisively abandoned human instruction and so received abundant wisdom from above, at an age when parents place children into the care of teachers and hand them over to schoolmasters, regardless of their own will, because they are so young. Within the inmost sanctuary, as though in a sublime palace, she was committed to God, as a living, royal throne, higher than any other, and provided with all the virtues appropriate to the great King who was to sit there.

This living shrine of the King of all ought not to be set before the eyes of all, as those words of Scripture also testify: "which no man can approach unto" (1 Tim. 6:16), meaning "which no man can see". Because, therefore, the tabernacle where the Most High rested on earth ought not to have the whole course of her life on show, the Virgin Mother desired to settle in the Holy of Holies immediately from infancy, the dwelling-place, as David calls it, of the holy name (Ps. 74:7). Where could be more fitting for her who was truly the holiest of all to dwell? Where else could be better for God's tent to be pitched? Surely it was absolutely necessary for the actual tabernacle to be set up in the same place as the figurative one? She was the tabernacle in which He who is seated above the whole creation rested, the true King, the Lord of all rulers, who is marvellously clad in the many-coloured kingly robe woven from both created and uncreated natures. His tabernacle does not shine with the brightness of precious metals, but because it is full of spiritual graces. It does not hold symbols of angels or the first-fruits of physical prototypes, but bears within it the inexpressible supernatural radiance of spiritual purity, a will conformed to God's, the divinely lovely brilliance of virginity, the magnificent lustre of all that is good and, to put it concisely, the place which truly held God who encompasses everything.

It was because Moses foresaw that she would be the living tabernacle who would hold God that he erected that other tabernacle, prepared that inmost sanctuary for her sake and, learning from God what would befall her, dignified it with sublimely exalted names, indicating to all in advance, by word and deed, the extraordinary, all-surpassing worthiness that would be hers from infancy. But the holy young Virgin did not take possession of this most fitting place from the beginning of her life – receiving as she did the honour of being God's tabernacle and living high above everyone else – solely because she outstripped all in the worthiness of her character, but also because, by so doing, she was presenting visible proof of the great mystery that would happen to her. For, strange as it seems, the holy Maid took as her home for several years the place assigned to God alone, which was consecrated as His dwelling, and out of which He gave audience at infrequent intervals to Moses, Aaron and those of their successors who were equally worthy, and where He was also believed to reside continuously between those encounters. In this way she made it clear, and declared in advance to as many as have understanding, that she was to be the true shrine and resting-place of God, an incomparably better mercy-seat for Him, and the divinely beautiful treasure-house of the highest pinnacle of the Spirit's mysteries.

In addition to what we have said, the Virgin was also silently making an important statement to the onlookers, that she was not being unreasonable in choosing to live in quietness and solitude. The Holy of Holies was out of sight of almost everyone, shut off from everybody, and protected by encircling walls and curtains, with veils and hangings before the entrances, which were never opened for anyone except the high priest according to the law, and only once a year for him, when he entered to gain God's mercy for himself and those outside (*cf.* Lev. 16:6, 11, 15). So how could the altar of the delight of the angels, the field in which the evergreen, or rather, eternal plant grows, the mercy-seat for the whole of mankind, into which the High Priest with the highest divine authority (Heb. 6:20; 7:26), the only one suitable for us, according to the apostle, entered once, and where He reconciled God to men and inseparably united them; how could this virginal treasure be kept anywhere else but in this innermost sanctuary, passing her life invisible to all?

If, according to the apostle, "the world was not worthy" even of the holy men of old, how could it deserve her who was higher than the saints of heaven? Understand also from this just how excellent the Virgin is. The former saints, when they fled from dwelling among men, were given, as the same apostle tells us, deserts, mountains and caves of the earth to live in (Heb. 11:38), whereas she was granted the Holy of Holies as her home. And the all-pure Virgin was allowed to go to live there even before she could be considered to have reached childhood, although she showed that she was more sensible than those who had attained to the age of reason, as we shall go on to demonstrate.

She was a gift from God, and to God, even before she was born – how could she be otherwise, as she was pre-ordained before all ages as the dwelling-place of the Maker of all worlds? She was a gift to God and the fruit of her righteous parents' vow and supplication – O the wings of that prayer! What boldness it found before the Lord! How spotless their hearts must have been to be able to offer up a prayer so far-reaching and effective! As the fruit of such a vow the Virgin was brought by her parents to the giver, like a beloved votive offering. (O finest of couples! O elect pair who cultivated and presented to God a dwelling-place dearer than heaven!) She was brought, like a most holy shoot sprung from a holy root, a shoot reaching from earth to heaven, so great was its honour, a shoot which would soon bring forth the pre-eternal, unfading flower, and was to produce Him by whose word alone everything natural and supernatural sprang to life. This shoot was led to be planted – Come forward, David, with your harp to express this in song – "Like a green olive tree in the house of God" (Ps. 52:8), "Like a tree", which will bear the perfection of God's mystery and will bring forth fruit inexplicably "by the rivers of water" of the Spirit (Ps. 1:3).

The Mother of God was led up to God by her parents, not as a young girl, nor as a child, nor just slightly younger than that, but as a three-year-old who had been weaned and taken from her mother's breast only a day or two before. But at that age she gave proof of discernment worthy of those capable of making sound decisions, for she was clearly seen to go forward with unspeakable joy. When they were already near the outer doors of the Temple, while noble young women, dressed in a fashion worthy of their race, were surrounding her with torches in their hands and eagerly escorting her in dignified procession, she demonstrated that she was more aware than anyone else of what was happening to her and what was going to take place. Solemn, graceful and admired, she was making her orderly way among the others, with a wonderfully calm bearing, manner and purpose defying description. Then, tempering decorum with eagerness and gently quickening her pace, she left behind the choir of virgins encircling her, taking the lead in front of them all, that it might become obvious that those words of the Psalm refer to her: "The virgins that follow her shall be brought unto the king. Her companions shall be brought with gladness and rejoicing: they shall be led into the king's temple" (Ps. 45:14–15 Lxx).

As soon as the high priest came out to meet her, and surely spoke that prophetic verse to her, "Hearken, O daughter, and consider, and incline thine ear; forget also thine own people, and thy father's house; so shall the king greatly desire thy beauty" (Ps. 45:10–11), she stopped reverently for a moment, then, on hearing these words, she rose up again. Immediately leaving everyone behind, her parents, nurses and contemporaries, she separated herself from the assembled company and went forward to the high priest, absolutely alone and full of joy. Turning her gracious and gentle gaze upon him, she affirmed with whatever gestures she could, and with childish murmurings, her wholehearted devotion to God.

How can these events fail to inspire amazement? The three-year-old puts herself into the hands of him who can direct her course in accordance with higher providence. She makes her own wise choice between nature and its Creator, and gives higher esteem to what is better. She chooses God instead of her mother and father's embrace, and prefers God's Temple and its high priest to being cosseted at home. Reckoning all these things worthless, but valuing God and everything pertaining to Him above all else, she ran gladly towards His Temple. Surely it was of her that David the prophet said to God, "Justice and judgment are the preparation of thy throne" (Ps. 89:14 Lxx), and "Righteousness and judgment are the achievement of his throne" (Ps. 97:2 Lxx). For she is styled the living throne of God, and in fact this honour belongs solely to her (because the word "throne" in the singular is not actually used of the bodiless, heavenly orders). It is through her rather than by means of those angelic Thrones that the foundation of great justice and ineffable righteousness came about and was revealed. So even before her birth the Virgin's discerning judgement was extolled, and now, before she had grown up, she publicly demonstrated its steadfastness.

Whereas Moses' tongue, although slow in other respects, nevertheless clearly proclaimed its own lack of discretion in his youth (Exod. 4:10), preserving traces of that flame, which is used, as the saying goes, for the testing of our mind's discernment, and the brightness of which is preferred to the radiance of gold. As for the other things we hear about him, to a certain extent they are good signs of his soul's future valour, but even these tokens are scarcely worthy of admiration compared to the events we are presently considering. For how could a kingly crown adorned with gold leaf and bright gems (cf. Exod. 28:36–29:6) appeal to a child's mentality as much as her mother's warm and loving embrace and appropriate care? Yet the Virgin voluntarily disdained these comforts. She ran towards God with unrestrainable love and persevered on her own in the inner sanctuary, as though continuously ministering to God in an indescribable way. Nothing of the sort ever happened to Moses. In his case it was fear rather than love for God which drove

him away from serving Pharaoh, and this when he was already on
the verge of manhood (Exod. 2:15). Later, however, after turning
his attention to virtue and struggling to acquire it, and after going
up the mountain to God, he was deemed worthy to be initiated
into the signs prefiguring the Virgin, and ceaselessly assisted in the
preparations for her.

Leaving Moses here below with the servants, together with
whom he appeared of course, let us turn to those who came to the
knowledge of God by themselves and of their own free will. Let
us admire Abraham and the far-famed Melchizedek, who turned
to God of their own accord – after they had already attained the
age of reason. They had observed that great proof pointing us to
God: this universe; the earth; what surrounds it; the combination
of elements; the noble harmony of opposites; the vast boundary
formed by the heavens which encircle the visible portion of
creation; the multitude of stars fixed therein; their varied and
wonderful disposition and their movement, which is neither simple
nor conflicting, but harmonious, orderly and lyrical; their progress
around their orbits; their conjunctions; their shared paths; their
alterations; the significant formations which result, according to
what experts in these matters tell us. These things and everything
else which happens according to nature's laws proclaim God who
is eternally above them.

The Virgin, by contrast, could not turn her eyes upon any of
these natural wonders – she was not old enough – yet she understood
God, and rejoiced as she was brought to Him. Or rather, she
approached of her own volition, as though it were natural for her
to wing her way towards holy and divine love. When God's high
priest saw that the Virgin had dwelling within her from infancy
such graces as hardly enter other people's souls in the fullest
prime of life, and then only if they are among the elect, and that
she would possess these gifts throughout her life in far greater
abundance than anyone else, he deemed her worthy of a more
excellent honour than could be granted to others. He led her into
the Holy of Holies and persuaded all those present to accept what
had come to pass with God's assistance and by His most righteous

decision. For she was to be His chosen vessel, not full of shadows and symbols like the ark, but full of truth. Unlike Paul who came after, she was not to bear God's Name before the Gentiles and kings (*cf.* Acts 9:15), but to carry in her womb Him whose name is Wonderful (Isa. 9:6), so much so that Paul, not Saul (*cf.* Acts 13:11), was made famous, second to none of the most eminent men of any age, because he was counted worthy to bear this name openly.

For this reason, if you give proper consideration not only to how any of the outstandingly virtuous men who ever lived started out, but also to the whole course of their struggle for virtue and even their final rewards and crowns from on high, you will find that they fall far short of the first steps of this child of God, which our entire race is now celebrating, commemorating with inexpressible joy her translation from human society into the Holy of Holies. Enoch, too, was taken away from among men (Gen. 5:24), but no public celebration is held for him. Later, Elijah was carried off in a fiery chariot (2 Kgs. 2:11), but he has not become the subject of such a great festival for the whole world, nor did divine bliss take hold of the universe and cause those in heaven to leap for joy with those on earth. After them, a three-year-old girl went to live somewhere else, and the whole world rejoiced and everything was filled with delight, overflowing with divine inspiration. Oh, how great a miracle is this! What power does this child possess? What consummate virtue and transcending majesty? Who is this girl who has overcome the world (*cf.* 1 John 5:4), transformed the human race, removed sadness – the fruit of our forefathers' curse – from mankind, and planted on earth this divine, incorruptible splendour, this joy we all share every year, which never grows old, blooms eternally, and is not subject to the passage of time, which puts an end to everything? But let us return again to our subject.

Enoch was translated because he pleased God. Once again, I will ignore the fact that he was three hundred and sixty-five years old and had reached the end of his life, whereas the child we are now considering was three years old when she started on spiritual works. From that time forward she inaugurated graces on earth, and then she immediately established her all-embracing renown, which reached from earth to heaven. God carried away Enoch too, but did He take him to heaven? Certainly not! For "no man hath ascended up to heaven, but he that came down from heaven", who for our sake was born a man like us of this Holy Virgin, "He who is in heaven" (John 3:13). If, however, it is written that Enoch was moved to somewhere on earth by God, he was clearly taken to a lesser place than that now allotted to the Virgin, for nowhere on earth is more sacred than the Holy of Holies. What happened to him brought no subsequent benefit to mankind. It did not wipe out sin, nor contribute to righteousness, because in the third generation after him that worldwide flood occurred (Gen. 5:21–32; 6:5ff). In the Virgin's time, however, and because of her, the renewal of the world came about. Through her, heaven threw open its gates once more, not to send forth raging torrents of terrible and destructive rain with every blast of wind, but the dew of the Spirit, sweetness for all our souls, the unapproachable light beyond our understanding (*cf.* 1 Tim. 6:16), "which lighteth every man that cometh into the world" (John 1:9).

If anyone draws attention to the fact that afterwards the Virgin went out among people, he should be aware that he is greatly enhancing her superiority. For as the only-begotten Son of the Father came down from the sanctuary of heaven for our sake, so she too came forth for our sake from the sanctuary of the Temple. The unwedded Bride of the immortal Father was betrothed to a mortal man, not because this was necessary for her, but to make known to us by means of witnesses the great miracle of her indescribable childbearing. The sun rises upon us at intervals and continuously moves around us in a circle, so that no one is hidden from its heat, according to the Scripture – "His going forth", it says, "is from the end of the heaven, and his circuit unto the ends of it" (Ps. 19:6), meaning, back to the point at which it came out. In the same way, the all-pure Virgin made her departure from mankind when she entered the Holy of Holies, then she went back among men, in order that, being pre-eminent in holiness, she might share the inalienable gift of hallowing with everyone. Nowhere was excluded, not even the world's secret places, that is to say, that innermost sanctuary.

As the effects of the sun upon us disappear, we need it to continue revolving around us time and time again. Since, however, the gifts bestowed by the Ever-Virgin are incorruptible, she only had to complete one circuit, and by so doing has brought never-ending illumination to all, causing to rise upon us, in a manner defying description, that Sun "with whom is no variableness, neither shadow of turning" (Jas. 1:17). So let us leave God's translation of Enoch, and turn the eyes of our understanding towards the taking up of Elijah, because he accomplished something better than Enoch, leaving his disciple the great gift of his mantle (2 Kgs. 2:13–14), through which Elisha did twice as many miracles. But the Virgin Mother's achievements were far superior to Elijah's. She herself became the wonder of wonders on earth, the greatest marvel of all time for the good of all. She also clothed God's Son Himself in Adam's garment from her womb, through which venerable garment we gained so many benefits that "if they should be written every one, I suppose that even the world itself could not contain the books that should be written", as the most theological of the evangelists tells us (John 21:25).

But why am I not weaving heavenly brightness into the Virgin's crown, instead of restricting myself to her radiant achievements on earth? Because she was going to give birth as a Virgin to Him whose nature is beyond all, her honour was all-surpassing from her earliest childhood, and incomparably more excellent even than the heavenly beings. To which angel were those words ever said, which were addressed to her while still an infant, "The king shall greatly desire thy beauty" (Ps. 45:11)? Did the angels not rather desire, according to the Scripture, to look into the things bestowed on us through her (cf. 1 Pet. 1:12)? Isaiah writes concerning the highest angelic orders, "And seraphims stood round about him" (Isa. 6:2 Lxx), whereas David, again, says of her, "Upon thy right hand did stand the queen" (Ps. 45:9). Do you see how they stand in different places? Learn from this the distinction between their ranks. The seraphim are round about God, but only the Queen of all is beside Him, she who is admired and extolled even by God Himself, who, as it were, proclaims her to the powers surrounding Him, saying, as it tells us in the Song of Songs, "How fair is my companion?" (cf. Song of Songs 4:1 Lxx). She is more radiant than light, richer in flowers than paradise, more beautifully adorned than the whole visible and invisible world. She is not just next to God, but, as is fitting, on His right hand. For where Christ took His seat in heaven, "on the right hand of the Majesty on high" (Heb. 1:3), she stands too, not just because she longs for Him, and is longed for in return, more than all others, even according to the dictates of nature, but because she is truly His throne. And where the King sits, there stands the throne.

Isaiah saw this throne in the midst of the choir of cherubim and said it was "high and lifted up" (Isa. 6:1), showing that the Mother of God is far exalted above the heavenly powers. If the highest order of the heavenly hierarchies were allotted second place immediately after her, still they are not second in order with regard to honour. Otherwise, although they would be inferior compared to her, she would only be slightly better than they, whereas now she is immeasurably superior to them. Just as we have no other luminary to put second after the sun's orb for abundance of light except the moon, even though it gives very little illumination, so, in the same way, there are no other divinely radiant beings which can be considered second to her except the seraphim. But to anyone who examines the matter carefully, the comparison will hardly appear worthy, as though a torch were being likened to a beacon visible far and wide. That is why the prophet presents the angels themselves glorifying God on her account, saying: "Blessed be the glory of the Lord from his throne" (cf. Ezek. 3:12). Elsewhere David, uniting in himself the masses of those being saved, and using the different voices of the various races, brought into harmony by her, strikes up that song so appropriate as a hymn, saying: "I will make thy name to be remembered in all generations: therefore shall the people praise thee for ever and ever" (Ps. 45:17).

Do you see how the whole creation gives thanks to the Virgin Mother, not in years gone by, but for ever and ever to endless ages? From this it can be understood that she too will never cease throughout the ages to do good to the whole creation, not just our own, but also to the immaterial, supernatural orders. For Isaiah gave clear proof that they, like us, only commune with, and touch, the intangible divine nature through her. He did not see the seraph taking the burning coal directly from the altar, but taking it by means of tongs, with which he also touched the prophet's lips and bestowed cleansing (cf. Isa. 6:6–7). The vision of the tongs is equivalent to the great vision seen by Moses of the burning bush which was not consumed (Exod. 3:2). Surely, everyone is aware that the Virgin Mother is both that burning bush and those tongs, as she conceived the divine fire without being consumed by fire. An archangel also ministered at that conception, and through her he united Him who takes away the sins of the world with the human race, thoroughly cleansing us by this union.

She alone forms the boundary between created and uncreated nature, and no one can come to God except through her and the mediator born of her, and none of God's gifts can be bestowed on angels or men except through her. As in the case with lamps on earth constructed of glass or some other transparent material, it is impossible to look at the light or enjoy its rays except through the lamp, so it is beyond the reach of all to look upwards to God or be helped by Him to make progress in any direction, except through the Ever-Virgin, this God-bearing lamp who is truly radiant with divine brightness. "God is in the midst of her", it says, "she shall not be moved" (Ps. 46:5).

If God requites us according to the measure of our love for Him, and he who loves the Son is loved by Him and by His Father, and becomes in a mysterious way the dwelling of both, as they make their home and walk in his soul, as the Lord promised (John 14:23, cf. 2 Cor. 6:16), who could love Him more than His Mother? For not only was He her only Son, but she bore Him on her own without a spouse, so her parental love was naturally double, not being shared with a partner. But who could be more beloved to the only-begotten Son than His Mother, particularly as He came forth in an indescribable way from her in the last times, just as He had come forth from the Father alone before all ages? And how could the honour due to her not be multiplied many times over, and above the fitting disposition of a son, by Him who came down to fulfil the law? If the love of the Father and the Son is one, and the honour and union bestowed by Both also comes from the Spirit – Oh, the Virgin's graces past understanding! – she bears within her soul the whole uncreated Trinity, one person of which she conceived without seed in her womb, and because she remained Virgin, gave birth to Him free from the pangs of childbirth.

Just as it was through her alone that He came to us, and "appeared on earth and lived among men" (Baruch 3:37), whereas previously He was invisible to all, so in the unending age that follows, any progress towards divine illumination, every revelation of the mysteries of the divine order, and every kind of spiritual gift is beyond the capacity of anyone, without her. Being the first to receive "the fulness of him that filleth all" (cf. Eph. 1:23), she brought Him within the grasp of all, sharing with each according to his strength and in proportion to the measure of his purity. Thus she is both the treasury and the treasurer of the riches of the Godhead, and the highest ranks of cherubim look to her and trust in her. They, above all others, are seized with longing for her, as, more than all others, they long for the outpouring of light and the granting of indescribable divine graces which come through her. All the spiritual powers under them share in due measure in this holy love, and in divine illumination through her. After them, for us too, for all men and women, according to the extent of our dispassionate and holy longing for this Godlike Virgin, immaterial, unceasing love and utterly sincere desire will be followed by the state of divine illumination and its clarity.

It is an eternal law in heaven that the lesser shall share by means of the greater in what lies beyond being. So, as the Virgin Mother is incomparably greater than all, as many as will share in God will do so through her, and as many as will know God will acknowledge her as the one who contained Him who cannot be contained, and as many as will extol God will hymn her, too, after Him. She is the reason for everything which preceded her, the protectress of everything which came after, and the cause of eternal blessings. She is the theme of the prophets, the starting-point of the apostles, the support of the martyrs, the foundation of teachers. She is the glory of those on earth, the delight of those in heaven, the adornment of the whole creation. She is the beginning, source and root of good things past telling, the summit and fulfilment of everything holy.

O Holy Virgin, how can I put everything about you into words? How can I express my desire? How can I glorify you, the treasure of glory? Just remembering you brings hallowing. A mere glance in your direction enlightens the mind, raising it instantly to divine heights. In you the eyes of our understanding become clear. In you our spirit is radiant with the presence of the divine Spirit. For you did not become the keeper and store of graces so as to have them for yourself, but to fill the universe with grace. For the person in charge of inexhaustible treasures oversees their distribution. Why would you shut away your wealth as it never diminishes? Share it abundantly with us, O Lady, and if we cannot contain it, enlarge our capacity, and then lavish it upon us. For you alone did not receive by measure, as all things were given into your hand.

May it be so. I think, however, that I should return to what I was saying and attempt to go on, if I may steal a glance into what lies within the sanctuary, bring it outside, extol it and expound it. May God assist me yet again. Because of the nature of speech, we are relying on something with very little power. The difficulties are many and great, and cannot be avoided, unless divine help from above is at hand. Let all of us who are followers of the ever-virgin Bride go forward, having prayed together that she would come to the aid of my words from the heavenly sanctuary where she now is. Let us enter the inner room, go together into the bridechamber and observe its secrets. For through her everything in heaven above and on earth below has been opened to us.

Let us see how types found fulfilment, how truth took perfect shape in the very place where it had been sketched out. She who is eternally the Holy of Holies entered the temporary Holy of Holies. The tabernacle, not made with hands, of the Word, the living human ark of the bread of life truly sent down to us from heaven, came into the place of the man-made ark, which contained the pot holding the manna (Heb. 9:4, *cf.* Exod. 16:31–34), which consisted of morning dew transformed by God's creative will into a type of food (*cf.* Num. 11:9). Because it came down from heaven, manna was called the bread of angels by those who were imperfect and uninitiated into truly divine mysteries, but to those wise in divine matters, who possessed foresight through the Holy Spirit, it was seen as a type of the Truth which was to come to pass in this Virgin. The book of life, which in an indescribable way received the imprint, not of words, but of the Word of the Father Himself, came into the place which had the tables of the covenant engraved with the lifeless form of words. The evergreen plant which bore the unfading flower which bestows incorruption on us, entered the place where Aaron's rod was kept, which symbolized, by sprouting buds without moisture, the future birth from the Virgin without seed.

Almost the whole Temple was covered in gold (1 Kgs. 6:20–22), and that inviolable ark was overlaid with pure gold (Exod. 25:11), and shone brilliantly on every side. Surely, therefore, the Virgin's beauty must have been brighter still, as God Himself desired it. Or do you wish to see a sign from heaven that this was so? Golden figures of angels stood around the ark, overshadowing it (Exod. 25:18–20). But angels themselves, not statues, surrounded this true ark and, what is more, they did not just keep watch but ministered to her, and served her with food. It is impossible to say what sort of nourishment it was, but it was far more wonderful than that highly-praised manna or the sustenance brought to Elijah (1 Kgs. 17:6). This is shown by the Scriptural account itself. When manna had been formed by God's command, it was carried by the air and fell like snow from above. David, the divine minstrel, recalled it and sang, "Man did eat angels' food" (Ps. 78:25), but he foresaw that it prefigured the truly heavenly nourishment of the Virgin. Whereas the air brought the manna and gave it every morning, an angel came every day with the

Virgin's food, as it was potent, full of mystery, proper to angels and akin to himself, and, naturally, as far superior to manna as angels are more excellent than air. As for Elijah, he was ministered to by a raven, a creature that hates children and is the symbol, they say, of lack of compassion for one's fellows.

The bringer of the Virgin's food is therefore a clear sign of her angelic way of life at this age. As was fitting, he continually served her without overshadowing her, and gave an indication of the great wonder that was to come to pass in her. It was not an angel that was to overshadow her, nor an archangel, nor even the cherubim and seraphim, but the power of the Highest in His very person (Luke 1:35). And what is more, the power of the Highest did not converse with her through a whirlwind and cloud (*cf.* Job 38:1), nor through darkness and fire (Heb. 12:18), nor through a gentle breeze (*cf.* 1 Kgs. 19:12 Lxx), as happened at sundry times to others who were deemed worthy, but it directly overshadowed her virgin womb without any kind of disguise. There was nothing between the one overshadowing and the one overshadowed, not air, either earthly or heavenly, nor anything perceptible or beyond our perception. Obviously this was union, not overshadowing. But as anything that overshadows something else naturally imprints its own shape and form upon it, it was not merely a union which came about in the Virgin's womb, but the formation of something. And what took shape from both, from the power of the Most High and this Most Holy Lady's virginal womb, was the Word of God made flesh. Oh, to what mysterious depths have we descended in our sermon!

But let us bring our address back from there (for it is obviously beyond the scope of mortal men and their minds to go so deep) and take up again the theme we have before us. The Virgin entered the Holy of Holies. At once she looked around and, when she saw that it pleased her, she felt it was a suitable place for her to stay. Through the beauty of what she saw, she immediately cast her mind's eye to unseen beauties, and no longer counted anything on earth delightful. Having risen above the needs of human nature and the pleasures of the senses, she decided that sights that are fair to look upon are not even worth seeing, and that things that are good to eat should be ignored. In this way, she was the first and only person to be shown to be in no danger from him who imposes his tyranny on us by these means, and in her turn she triumphed over him. She did not struggle with him just from morning until evening, nor just concerning the fruit of one plant (Gen. 3:2–9), but for the space of many years in respect of all the various pleasures invented by the powers of darkness as bait to catch souls. This holy Maid, alone of mankind, utterly despised all these delights while still an infant, and as a reward was rightly brought food from heaven by an angel, by which she was physically strengthened, and which served as a testimony that her way of life was worthy of heaven. In fact, if I may say something highly fitting and appropriate to the dignity of the ever-virgin Bride, right from the beginning she was shown to be the Queen of heaven, as she had heavenly beings to wait upon her.

She lived, as though in paradise, in a place removed from the earth, or rather, as though in the courts of heaven, for that sanctuary was a symbol of those courts. Thus she led an unencumbered life without cares or occupation, free from sorrow, with no share in base passions, above that pleasure which is inseparable from pain. She lived for God alone and was sustained and preserved only by Him who was to pitch His tent among us through her. Obviously she saw only God, making God her delight and continually waiting on Him.

With profound understanding she listened to the writings of Moses and the revelations of the other prophets when, every Saturday, all the people gathered outside, as the law ordained. She learnt about Adam and Eve and everything that happened to them: how they were brought out of non-being, settled in paradise, and given a commandment there; about the evil one's ruinous counsel, and the resulting theft; about their expulsion from paradise on that account, the loss of immortality, and the change to this way of life full of pain. In addition, she saw that as time passed, life continued under the inherited curse and grew ever worse, God's creature made in His image was estranged from the Creator and became more and more closely associated with the one who had evilly schemed to crush him. (Alas for the evil one's power over us and his insatiable rage against us! Woe to our insensitivity and our inclination to return to the earth!) No one was capable of putting an end to this impulse which brings destruction on all men alike, or to the uncheckable rush of our race towards hell. When the Holy Virgin Maid heard and understood this, she was filled with pity for humanity and, with the aim of finding a remedy to counteract this great affliction, she resolved at once to turn with her whole mind to God. She took it upon herself to represent us, to constrain Him who is above compulsion, and quickly draw Him towards us, that He might remove the curse from among us, halt the advance of the fire burning men's souls, weaken our enemies, answer our prayers, shine upon us with light that never sets and, having healed our sickness, unite His creature with Himself.

Having thought over these things so relevant to her, the Virgin full of grace interceded for all humanity in an amazing way defying description. Seeking to converse persuasively and honestly with God, to whom she came as a self-appointed ambassador, or rather as one ordained by Him, she eagerly examined every type of virtue, those proclaimed in the law and those discovered by reason, and by men devoted to both. She considered every aspect of each of the principal branches of learning as though they were impressions left by a seal, her intention being to discover which was most akin to God and which had taken its imprint from Him and was therefore capable of impressing His image on its adherents, wiping out the marks made by material concerns. Since the Virgin recognized that nothing revealed by men before her time went this far, she inaugurated something better and more perfect. She invented, put into practice, and handed down to those who came after her, a practice higher than any vision, and a vision as far superior to that which was formerly so highly acclaimed as the truth is superior to imagination.

The greatness of this mystery can be briefly stated. I shall utter words which are beneficial to all Christians, but especially to those who have renounced the world. Through what I say you may be able to taste those good things to come, to stand with angels and become a citizen of heaven, since you wish to emulate as far as possible the ever-virgin Bride who was the first and only person to forsake the world from infancy for the world's sake. The goodness she practised while shut away encompassed every kind of virtue: all those which had been discovered before her time and were openly bestowed on those men we have mentioned, and adorned their characters, and by means of which domestic and civic affairs were well managed. The other aspect of the Virgin, however, superior to what we have recounted, is entirely knowledge, through which we may search out natural principles and, as far as lies within our grasp, contemplate the analogies, figures and quantities of the soul and things which are inseparably separable from matter.

Let us consider, from a theological and philosophical point of view, things completely free from matter, a subject which the Greeks, or rather the fathers and patrons of the art, called the first philosophy, being unaware of any higher kind of contemplation. Even this, although it contains some truth, is as far removed from the vision of God, and as different from converse with Him, as possessing is distinct from knowing. Saying something about God is not the same as encountering Him. Speaking of God requires that you pronounce words, and perhaps that you have some skill with them, if you are not just to have knowledge but to make use of it and pass it on. It also requires all sorts of logical reasoning, compelling arguments and worldly examples, all or most of which are gathered by seeing and hearing, and are the prerogative of people who spend their lives in this world. They may be acquired by the wise men of this present age, even though their lives and souls may not be completely pure. It is absolutely impossible, however, to truly encounter God unless, in addition to being cleansed, we go outside, or rather, beyond ourselves, leaving behind everything perceptible to our senses, together with our ability to perceive, and being lifted up above thoughts, reason, and every kind of knowledge, above even the mind itself, and wholly given over to the energy of spiritual perception, which Solomon calls divine awareness (*cf.* Prov. 2:3–5 Lxx), we attain to that unknowing which lies beyond knowledge, that is to say, above every kind of much-vaunted philosophy, even though the purpose of the most excellent part of philosophy is knowledge.

Seeking after this – for it is absolutely necessary for ambassadors to meet those to whom they have been sent – the Virgin found that holy stillness was her guide: stillness, in which the mind and the world stand still (*cf.* Ps. 46:10), forgetfulness of the things below, initiation into the things above, the laying aside of ideas for something better. This is true activity, a means of approaching contemplation or, to state it more aptly, the vision of God, which is the only proof of a soul in good health. Every other virtue is like healing medicine for the soul's illnesses and the evil passions which have put down roots in it through sloth. Contemplation, by contrast, is the fruit of a healthy soul; it aims to achieve a certain end and is of a kind that deifies; for it is through contemplation that a person is made divine, not by speculative analogies on the basis of skilful reasoning and observations – perish the thought (for that would be something base and human) – but under the guidance of stillness. Continuing in our life's upper room, as it were, in prayers and supplications night and day (*cf.* Acts 1:13–14), in some way we touch that blessed nature that cannot be touched.

Thus those whose hearts have been purified by holy stillness, inasmuch as they have been ineffably permeated by the light that transcends both sense and mind, see God within themselves as in a mirror (*cf.* 2 Cor. 3:18). The immediate proof of this is the Virgin, who, having kept company with quietness from the earliest age, brings the greatest benefits to us, and commends to God those in need as no one else can. She alone lived in holy quiet from such early childhood in a manner surpassing nature, and she alone of the human race bore the Word, who is the God-man, without knowing man.

We must, however, return to our subject in order to make this great principle easy for "those who have ears" to grasp (*cf.* Mark 4:23; 7:16). I admire that type of eulogy which benefits the hearers by revealing to them the way of salvation. And even if it is the case that some of the phrases are difficult to understand and cannot easily be comprehended by those whose minds lack concentration, I do not think such words should be banished from the holy precincts; for we do not avoid the narrow way which leads to life simply because it is difficult to follow (*cf.* Matt. 7:14). Onward then, my brave companions, as many of you as do not prefer easily-earned dust to hard-won gold, and let each of you gather his mind within itself, just as men going along narrow passageways gather up their cloaks, and ascend intently towards the majesty of this thought; for there is no accessible means of ascent to so highly exalted a meaning for those who creep along the ground. Once, however, you have lifted your minds above material concerns and resolved to meditate on the Mother of God's divine way of life in the holy sanctuary, eager to understand something of what happened there and to emulate her as far as possible, then perhaps you will soon receive that blessed gift of those purified in heart (*cf.* Matt. 5:8), and invisibly observe the honours proper to the immortal world.

Man, the greater world contained in a lesser, is the combination of all things, the recapitulation of God's creation, which is why he was produced last of all, just as we put an epilogue at the end of speeches; in fact, you could say that this universe is the composition of the person of the Word Himself. Man, then, brings his mind and senses into unity with the greater wisdom of Him who is able to mingle elements that cannot be mixed, by using his imagination, opinion and thought as intermediaries, as genuine bonds of the extremes. Something similar occurs with the four perceptible elements which make up the world around us: air mediates between fire and water, and water between air and earth, and thus opposites are bound together, and peace is established between conflicting elements, without them in any way losing their mutually repelling properties. Thus it is with the world, which is great in size; thus it is with man, who is great in honour. In this way, man and the world are in communion with each other, but whereas the world is greater than man in magnitude, man transcends it in intelligence. He is stored up like treasure within the world, like a very precious object kept in a large house and worth much more than the building that contains it. Or like many-coloured, costly royal robes (not like the king himself, for this honour has been lost) within the palace, where the palace is made of stones which, though huge, can be bought cheaply by anyone, whereas royal robes are made with small but precious stones which are hard to come by.

How much greater is the mind than the heavens! It is the image of God, knows God, and alone of everything on earth can, if it wishes, become God, exalting man's humble body at the same time. How much more excellent are man's senses than the earth! They can comprehend not just the earth's dimensions, its bulk and its various qualities, but ascend through knowledge to the heavenly spheres, understand their various movements, be aware of all the various and perhaps significant ways in which stars come together and separate, and thus lay the foundation, as it were, for the science of astronomy. Even the things in between the heavens and the earth are worth less than what lies on the boundary between man's mind and his senses, for although they serve the same purpose in our analogy, in context, they are as different as can be. Man's senses are a non-rational power, capable of knowing and comprehending perceptible objects when they are present. Imagination has its starting point in the senses, but exercises its abilities even in the absence of objects which can be perceived by the senses. It could perhaps also be called mind, in so far as it can act without such objects; although as not existing outside divisible things, it is passive. Opinions originating from the imagination are irrational judgements, but not those which come from reasoning; for the ability to form opinions is natural to both. Man's reasoning is always logical, and comes eventually, by means of a gradual process, to opinions in accordance with reason. All these mental powers were formed, and act, by means of the primary organ, man's natural spirit within the brain. The mind, by contrast, has no organ, but is an essence complete in itself, able to operate independently, even though it lowers itself to the level of man's natural life which develops through reasoning.

But why have I set out these divisions and distinctions now? Why did I first enumerate the types of virtues, then afterwards the soul's powers? Because the seeds of those virtues come from these faculties, and their whole existence stems from them. Since, therefore, the divinely wise Virgin could not reap from the virtues the closest possible relationship to God, she investigated the soul's capabilities, to see whether she might perhaps discover a means of attaining to oneness with Him. Some of them she found to be completely irrational and incapable of rising above things perceptible to the senses. As for the capacity to form opinions and concepts, although these are rational powers, they are not detached from that storehouse of the senses, the imagination, and what is more they also function through the organ of man's natural spirit. She prudently understood what the apostle, too, said later: "The natural man receiveth not the things of the Spirit of God" (1 Cor. 2:14). She therefore looked for something higher, a truly spiritual life unadulterated with earthly concerns, and, in a way which goes beyond the limitations of created nature, she longed for God and heavenly union with Him. Just as it is impossible to desire visible light without desiring the sun, so it was with her.

She found that the purest thing in us, the only perfect and indivisible essence that we have, is precisely intended by nature for this holy and divine love. As the greatest power of the soul, the mind defines and unifies even those processes of reason upon which the things pertaining to the sciences are based, which creep forward almost like reptiles, together or individually, making inferences and interpretations. Although the mind can come down to the level of human reasoning, and by it to a life full of complexities, since its energies are available for all, yet it indubitably has another, superior mode of operation, which it is capable of putting into action by itself. For it is able to remain on its own, either when separated from the body and the things pertaining to the body, or when, although still bound to it, it is enabled, by means of diligence, and assisted by divine grace, to leave behind this varied, complex and lowly way of living. It is like a rider, who is certainly capable of activity eminently superior to merely holding the reins, and could put it into effect on his own, not only if he were to dismount, but even on horseback or in a chariot, had he not deliberately devoted his entire attention simply to guiding the horse. In the same way, if the mind did not wholly revolve without ceasing around base concerns, it could be given over to superior, more exalted activity, namely, that which is proper to it, and which is the sole means by which it can enter into union with God. This is, however, far more difficult, because it is by nature intertwined with the body, and entangled with material knowledge and all the different ties that bind this life to earthly matters, and are hard to lay aside.

The all-pure Virgin threw off those ties from the very beginning of her life, and withdrew from people. She escaped from a blameworthy way of life, and chose to live in solitude out of sight of all, inside the sanctuary. There, having loosed every bond with material things, shaken off every tie and even risen above sympathy towards her own body, she united her mind with its turning towards itself and attention, and with unceasing holy prayer. Having become her own mistress by this means, and being established above the jumble of thoughts in all their different guises, and above absolutely every form of being, she constructed a new and indescribable way to heaven, which I would call silence of the mind. Intent upon this silence, she flew high above all created things, saw God's glory more clearly than Moses (cf. Exod. 33:18–23), and beheld divine grace, which is not at all within the capacity of men's senses, but is a gracious and holy sight for spotless souls and minds. Partaking of this vision, she became, according to the sacred hymnographers, a radiant cloud of the truly living water, the dawn of the mystical day, and the fiery chariot of the Word.

Without the visitation of divine grace, even if a mind were to discover divine awareness (cf. Prov. 2:3–5 Lxx), it could not see anything or act on its own, just as the eye can do nothing without visible light. To those who are eternal, that is to say, to those who are like God, He is nothing but light, and as the sun is to visible objects, so God is to what the mind perceives. Man's sight, when it is in action, itself becomes light, communes with the light and sees with the light, and the first thing it beholds is this light poured out on everything visible. In exactly the same way, anyone fortunate enough to attain to the divine energy, and to undergo divine transformation, himself becomes completely like the light, is with the light, and by means of the light sees clearly things which, were it not for this great and inexpressible grace, would be invisible to all; for it is beyond not only the bodily senses, but also everything that can be known by us, and indeed it is invisible even to those who surpass us in natural power. According to the Lord's Beatitude, which cannot prove false, those whose hearts have been purified see God (Matt. 5:8), who, in the words of the great theologian, John, the son of thunder, is light (1 John 1:5), and dwells in, and reveals Himself to, those who love Him, and are loved by Him, in accordance with His own promise to them (cf. John 14:23). He appears to the purified mind as though in a mirror (cf. 2 Cor. 3:18), although in Himself He is invisible. For such is the form reflected in a mirror: it appears but cannot be seen, and it is utterly impossible for anyone to see the reflection in the mirror and at the same time the object being reflected. This is how God is seen now by those cleansed by divine love, but then, it says, they shall see Him "face to face" (1 Cor. 13:12).

But who ever loved God more than she, whom we now praise? And who was ever loved by God more than she? What other creature could ever be purer than she, or equal to her in purity, or anywhere near as pure? For this reason, she alone of all mankind throughout the ages was initiated into the highest mysteries by these divine visions, was united in this way with God, and became like Him. She then accomplished the super-human rôle of intercessor on our behalf, and brought it to perfection through herself, not just acquiring the exaltation of mind that lies beyond reason, but using it for the sake of us all, and achieving this great and surpassingly great deed by means of her boldness towards God. For she did not merely come to resemble God, but she also made God in the likeness of man, not just by persuading Him, but by conceiving Him without seed and bearing Him in a way past telling. Having been fashioned by God through grace – which is why she was addressed as "thou that art full of grace" by the archangel – she shaped God in human form – which is why she was given the good tidings with the greeting, "Rejoice" (Luke 1:28).

"Who shall tell of your mighty acts, O Virgin, or who can show forth all your praise, whose child is divine?" (cf. Ps. 106:2). You became the Mother of God. You have united the mind with God. You have joined God with flesh. You have made God the Son of man, and man the son of God. You have reconciled the world to the Creator of the world. By your deeds, you have taught us that visions do not come to those who are truly human through their senses alone, or even through their thoughts – for then they would be little better than beasts – but much more by means of the purification of the mind and by participation in divine grace, through which we shall delight in the divine beauties, not by thoughts but by immaterial contact.

You have enabled us, through our very senses, to see Him who is invisible in our own human form and shape, and, by touching matter, to touch the immaterial and intangible one. You gave human nourishment to Him who nurtures the angels. Through Him who provides for the angels you have fed us on the truly heavenly and incorruptible food. You have made men live the same life as angels, or rather, you have made them worthy of greater privileges, in that you conceived, of the Holy Spirit, the theandric Form, and mysteriously gave Him birth, linking man's nature to the divine nature and rendering it, as it were, equally divine (*cf.* Heb. 10:12), in inexpressible fashion.

They say there was a king called Pious, and it seems he was named after his deeds. It is related of him that once, when those around him were suffering from thirst, he lifted up his just right hand to God, saying, "With this hand I entreat you, O giver of life, for with it I have never taken a life", and immediately rainclouds appeared overhead from the sky, and torrential rain fell. The Virgin, however, the Queen of the truly pious, lifted up her mind in the Holy of Holies, utterly withdrawn from everything below or, more accurately, never having been attached to such things at all, and, saying to God, "I beseech You with this mind, which nothing earthly has ever entered", made the whole world heaven. She did not call upon clouds, which have obeyed many people on numerous occasions through prayer, but upon Him who brings the clouds from the ends of the earth. She did not bring us temporary relief through rain, but brought us the Treasure of all goodness, the everlasting fount that springs without ceasing from the Father's bosom, the Word who is seated above the vaults of heaven. Thence He has brought us living water, and bestowed on us food which makes those who partake of it immortal and sons of God, not adopted merely in name, but in the fellowship of the Holy Spirit – O ineffable gift! – brought close to God and one to another through God's flesh and blood.

Let us therefore preserve this unity with God and one another, which has been divinely wrought within us by God through the ordinances of love. Let us always look to our heavenly Father. Let us forsake the world, for we are no longer of the earth, earthy, like the first man, but like the second man, the Lord, from heaven (1 Cor. 15:47). Let us lift up our hearts to Him. Let us contemplate this magnificent spectacle, our nature dwelling eternally with the immaterial fire of the Godhead. And putting aside our coats of skins (cf. Gen. 3:21), in which we were clothed as a result of transgression, let us stand in the holy place, each of us marking out his own holy ground through virtue and by turning unswervingly towards God, that, as God dwells in fire, we may have boldness to run towards Him and be enlightened and, once illumined, to live with Him in the glory of His sublime light, the radiance of three suns and one sovereignty.

To whom belong all glory, dominion, honour and worship, now and unto unceasing ages. Amen.

On the Annunciation

WHEN THE PROPHET AND PSALMIST was enumerating the different aspects of Creation and observing God's wisdom in them all, he was filled with amazement and cried out while writing, "O Lord, how manifold are thy works! In wisdom hast thou made them all" (Ps. 104:24). Now that I am attempting, if I can, to tell you about the manifestation in the flesh of the Word Who made all things, what fitting word of praise will I find? If all things that exist inspire wonder, and their coming out of non-being into being is something divine and greatly to be hymned, how much more amazing, divine and demanding of our praises is it for a being to become god, and not just god, but the God Who truly is? Especially as it was our nature which was neither able nor willing to preserve the image in which it was made, and had therefore been rightly banished to the lower parts of the earth. That our nature should become like God, and that through it we should receive the gift of returning to what is better, is a mystery so great and divine, so ineffable and beyond understanding, that it remained absolutely unrecognized by holy angels and men, and even by the prophets, although they had spiritual vision, and was hidden throughout the ages. But why am I speaking about the time before it was accomplished? Even now it has happened, how it happened, although not the fact that it has, remains a mystery, believed not known, worshipped not investigated, and only believed and worshipped through the Spirit. "No man can say that Jesus is Lord, but by the Holy Ghost" (1 Cor. 12:3), and the Apostle tells us that it is through the Spirit that we worship and pray (Rom. 8:26).

The event which we celebrate today clearly proves that this mystery is beyond the understanding not only of men but of Angels and even Archangels. The Archangel brought the Good Tidings to the Virgin that she would conceive (Luke 1:26–38). But when she sought to find out the way it would happen and asked him, "How shall this be, seeing I know not a man" (Luke 1:34), the Archangel was completely unable to explain how. He took refuge in God, saying, "The Holy Ghost shall come upon thee, and the power of the Highest shall overshadow thee" (Luke 1:35). It was as if someone had asked Moses, "How was man formed out of the ground? How were bones, nerves and flesh made out of dust, or the senses out of what is insensate? Or how was another human being created from Adam's rib? How was the bone stretched out, divided up, joined and fastened together? How were the internal organs, the various juices and everything else formed from a bone?" If someone had asked these questions of Moses all he would have said was that it was God Who took dust from the ground and formed Adam, and took of Adam's ribs and made Eve. He would have said Who the Creator was, but not the way in which these things were done. In the same way, Gabriel said that the Holy Spirit and the power of the Highest would bring about the Birth without seed, but he did not say how. He went on to mention that Elizabeth, who was barren, had conceived in her old age, and all he could say was that with God nothing was impossible (Luke 1:35–37). So how could he explain how she was to conceive and bear a child in virginity?

Nevertheless, the Archangel's words to the Virgin did contain something more, a reference to a greater mystery. "The Holy Ghost", he said, "shall come upon thee, and the power of the Highest shall overshadow thee" (Luke 1:35). Why was this? Because the child to be born was not to be called a prophet or simply a man, like Adam, but the Son of the Highest, Saviour, Deliverer of the human race and eternal King. When stones fall away from the peak of a mountain and go right down to the foot, many overhanging crags are left in their place. In the same way, when in paradise we fell away from the divine commandment and the blessed and godly way of life, and were brought down as far as Hades, many evils resulted. Not only did the ground yield visible thorns and thistles in accordance with the curse upon our Forefather, but we, to an even greater extent, were sown with the thorns of all sorts of evil passions and with sin's dreadful thistles. Our race did not receive just that sorrow allotted to our First Mother by the curse which condemned her to bear children in sorrow (Gen. 3:16), but almost all our life became pain and sorrow.

However, God Who made us looked lovingly down on us in His mercy. He bowed the heavens and came down. Having taken our nature upon Him from the Holy Virgin, He renewed and restored it. Or rather, He led it up to divine and heavenly heights. Wishing to achieve this, to bring to fulfilment on this day His pre-eternal counsel, He sent the Archangel Gabriel, as Luke the Evangelist tells us, "to Nazareth, to a virgin espoused to a man whose name was Joseph, of the house of David; and the virgin's name was Mary" (Luke 1:26–27).

God sent the Archangel to a virgin and made her, who continued a virgin, His mother by means of a salutation alone. If He had been conceived from seed, He would not have been a new man, nor sinless, nor the Saviour of sinners. The flesh's impulse to reproduce is not subject to our minds, which God has appointed to govern us, and is not altogether without sin. That is why David said, "I was shapen in iniquity; and in sin did my mother conceive me" (Ps. 51:5). So if the conception of God had been from seed, He would not have been a new man, nor the Author of new life which will never grow old. If He were from the old stock and inherited its sin, He would not have been able to bear within Himself the fullness of the incorruptible Godhead or to make His Flesh an inexhaustible Source of sanctification, able to wash away even the defilement of our First Parents by its abundant power, and sufficient to sanctify all who came after them. That is why neither an angel nor a man came to save us, but the Lord Himself, Who was conceived and took flesh in the womb of a virgin, while remaining unchanged as God.

It was necessary for the Virgin to have a witness to the conception without seed, and a helper in those events which were to be accomplished in accordance with the divine dispensation. What were these? The journey to Bethlehem, where the Birth took place (Luke 2:1–7), proclaimed and glorified by the heavenly angels (Luke 2:8–14). The entry into the Temple, where Simeon and Anna bore witness that the Infant was the Lord of life and death (Luke 2:22–38). The flight into Egypt to escape Herod, and the return from Egypt in accordance with the holy prophesies (Matt. 2:13–21; Hos. 11:1; cf. Exod. 4:19), and all the other events which we cannot now relate. On account of these, Joseph was taken as her betrothed, and the angel was sent "to a virgin espoused to a man whose name was Joseph" (Luke 1:26–27). You should understand the reference to being "of the house and lineage of David" as applying to them both (Luke 2:4; cf. 1:27). For both the Virgin and Joseph traced their families back to David.

"And the virgin's name", it says, "was Mary" (Luke 1:27), which means "Lady". This shows the Virgin's dignity, how certain was her virginity and set apart was her life, exact in every respect and completely blameless. She properly bore the name of Virgin, and possessed to the full all the attributes of purity. She was a virgin in both body and soul, and kept all the powers of her soul and her bodily senses far above any defilement. This she did authoritatively, steadfastly, decisively and altogether inviolably at all times, as a closed gate preserves the treasures within, and a sealed book keeps hidden from sight what is written inside. The Scriptures say of her, "This is the sealed book" (cf. Rev. 5:1–6:1; Dan. 12:4) and "this gate shall be shut, and no man shall enter in by it" (Ezek. 44:2).

The Virgin is also duly called "Lady" in another sense, as she has the mastery of all things, having divinely conceived and borne in virginity the Master of all by His nature. Yet she is the Lady not just because she is free from servitude and a partaker of divine power, but because she is the fount and root of the freedom of the human race, especially after the ineffable and joyful Birth. A married woman is ruled over rather than being a lady, especially after sorrowful and painful childbirth, in accordance with that curse on Eve: "In sorrow thou shalt bring forth children; and thy desire shall be to thy husband, and he shall rule over thee" (Gen. 3:16). Freeing the human race, the Virgin Mother received through the angel joy and blessing instead of this curse. "And the angel came in to her", it says, "and said, Hail, thou that art highly favoured, the Lord is with thee: blessed art thou among women" (Luke 1:28). The Archangel was not foretelling the future by saying, "The Lord is with thee", but was declaring what he saw happening invisibly at that time. Perceiving that divine and human gifts of grace were to be found in her, and that she was adorned with all the gifts of the holy Spirit, he truly proclaimed her full of grace. He saw that she had already received to dwell within her the One in Whom are all these treasures of grace. He saw in advance the painless pregnancy and the Birth without labour, and announced to her that she should rejoice, and affirmed that she alone was rightly blessed and glorified among women. Even if other women may be extolled, no other can be magnified with the surpassing glory of the Virgin Mother of God.

When the Virgin saw the Archangel she was afraid lest he be a deceitful messenger beguiling unwary women like Eve, and she did not accept his greeting unquestioningly. As she did not yet clearly perceive the bond with God which the Archangel was announcing to her, "she was troubled", it says, "at his saying". She was utterly determined to hold fast to her virginity, "and cast in her mind what manner of salutation this should be" (Luke 1:29). So the Archangel dispelled the godly fear of the Virgin full of grace by telling her, "Fear not, Mary: for thou hast found favour with God" (Luke 1:30). What favour? "That grace which is only possible for Him Who can do the impossible, and which has been kept for you alone from before the ages." "Behold, thou shalt conceive in thy womb" (Luke 1:31). "When you hear about conception", he told her, "do not suppose that there will be any deviation from virginity. You must not be anxious or troubled on that account." For these words, "Behold, thou shalt conceive", spoken to her who is a virgin, show that the conception is to accompany virginity.

"Behold, thou shalt conceive", he said, "and bring forth a son" (Luke 1:31). Continuing as you are now with your virginity inviolate, you shall conceive a child and bear the Son of the Highest. Isaiah foresaw this many years before and prophesied, "Behold, a virgin shall conceive, and bear a son" (Isa. 7:14), and, "I went unto the prophetess" (Isa. 8:3). In what way did the Prophet go to the Prophetess? In the same way as the Archangel now came to her. What the Archangel now saw, the Prophet foresaw and foretold. That the Virgin was a prophetess with the gift of prophecy, is proved to all by her hymn to God in the Gospel (Luke 1:46–55).

It says that Isaiah went to the Prophetess, wholly in the spirit of prophecy, and she conceived. Before the pain of labour arrived, she fled and bore a male child (Isa. 8:3–4). The Archangel now told the Virgin, "Thou shalt bring forth a son, and shalt call his name Jesus" – which means "Saviour" – "He shall be great" (Luke 1:31). Again, Isaiah's words were, "Wonderful, Counsellor, Mighty One, Governor, Prince of Peace, Father of the age to come" (Isa. 9:6 Lxx). In harmony with this, the Archangel now said, "He shall be great, and shall be called the Son of the Highest" (Luke 1:32). (Why did he say, "He shall be", and, "shall be called", and not, "He is great and is the Son of the Highest"? Because he was referring to the humanity of Christ). The Archangel disclosed at the same time that He would be known to all and proclaimed by all to be great and the Son of the Highest, so that later Paul could say, "God was manifest in the flesh, preached unto the Gentiles, believed on in the world" (1 Tim. 3:16). The Archangel continued, "The Lord God shall give unto him the throne of his father David: and he shall reign over the house of Jacob for ever; and of his kingdom there shall be no end" (Luke 1:32–33). He Whose kingdom is eternal and without end is God. But the Child to be born also had David as His father, therefore He was also man. He was both God and man,

Son of man and Son of God. As man He received the inalienable kingdom from God the Father, as Daniel saw and announced beforehand: "I beheld till the thrones were set in place, and the Ancient of days did sit, and, behold, one like the Son of man came with the clouds of heaven, and came to the Ancient of days. And there was given him dominion, and glory, and his kingdom is an everlasting kingdom, which shall not be taken by any other king" (Dan. 7:9; Dan. 7:13–14 Lxx).

He was to sit upon the throne of David and reign over the house of Jacob. Jacob was the patriarch of all God-fearing people, whereas David was the first to prefigure Christ by reigning in the fear of God and in a way pleasing to Him. Christ brought together patriarchate and kingship into one heavenly and earthly dominion. As soon as the highly favoured Virgin heard those extraordinary divine words addressed to her by the Archangel, "The Lord is with thee" (Luke 1:28), and, "Behold, thou shalt conceive, and bring forth a son, the Son of the Highest who shall reign for ever" (*cf.* Luke 1:31–33), she replied, "How shall this be unto me, seeing I know not a man?" (*cf.* Luke 1:34). "Although you bring spiritual tidings far above the passions of the flesh, you speak to me of conception in the womb, being with Christ and childbirth, and you emphasize the mention of conception by adding the word 'Behold'." "How shall this be unto me", she said, "seeing I know not a man?"

The Virgin did not say this because she disbelieved, but because she wanted to find out as much as possible about the matter. Therefore the Archangel told her, "The Holy Ghost shall come upon thee, and the power of the Highest shall overshadow thee: therefore also that holy thing which shall be born of thee shall be called the Son of God" (Luke 1:35). "You are holy", he says, "and full of grace, O Virgin. However, the Holy Spirit shall again come upon you, preparing and completing the work of God within you by the bestowal of a higher sanctification. The power of the Highest shall overshadow you, to strengthen you, and by overshadowing you and uniting you with itself, shall form the humanity of the One to be born of you, that He may be holy, the

Son of God and the power of the Highest in the shape of a man. And behold, your kinswoman Elizabeth, who has been barren all her life, is now mysteriously with child in her old age, by the will of God, for with God nothing shall be impossible."

How did the highly favoured Virgin, with her unrivalled and holy understanding, respond to these words? She ran to God and reached out to Him in prayer, saying to the Archangel, "If, as you tell me, the Holy Spirit shall come upon me, purifying my nature still further and strengthening me to receive the unborn Saviour; if the power of the Highest shall overshadow me, forming Him Who is in the form of God as man within me and bringing about a Birth without seed; if the holy Child which shall be born is to be the Son of God and God and the everlasting King, since with God nothing is impossible", "Behold the handmaid of the Lord; be it unto me according to thy word" (Luke 1:38). And the angel departed from her, leaving the Maker of all united with a body within her womb. By means of this union, which was the object of his ministry, he had procured salvation for the world. Isaiah clearly revealed all this beforehand by what he was so blessed as to be counted worthy to experience. He did not see the Seraphim take the live coal directly off the heavenly, spiritual altar. The Seraphim took it with tongs, and it was by means of these that he touched the Prophet's lips to purify him (Isa. 6:5–7). The tongs were the same as the burning bush which was not consumed by the fire, in that great vision seen by Moses (Exod. 3:2–6).

Surely it is obvious to anyone that the Virgin Mother is both the burning bush and the tongs. She conceived the divine fire within her and was not burnt, and an Archangel ministered at the conception, and through her the Bearer of the sins of the world was united with the human race, purifying us thoroughly by means of this indescribable bond. The Virgin Mother, and she alone, is the frontier between created and uncreated nature. All who know God will recognize her as the one who contained Him Who cannot be contained. All who sing hymns to God will praise her next after Him. She is the cause of the benefits which preceded her, the protectress of those which came after, and through her those good things which are eternal shall be received. She is the theme of the prophets, the first of the Apostles, the support of the martyrs, the dais of the teachers. She is the glory of those on earth, the delight of those in heaven, the adornment of the whole Creation. She is the beginning, fount and root of the hope stored up for us in heaven.

To which may we all attain by her prayers for us, to the glory of Him Who was begotten of the Father before all ages, and, in these last times, became incarnate of her, even Jesus Christ Our Lord. To Whom belong all glory, honour and worship, now and for ever and unto the ages of ages. Amen.

On the Mother of God as First to See the Risen Christ

THE RESURRECTION OF THE LORD is the renewal of human nature, and the renewal, re-creation and return to immortality of the first Adam who was swallowed up by death because of sin, and through death went back to the earth from which he was formed. In the beginning nobody saw Adam being made and brought to life, for no one existed yet at that time. However, once he had received the breath of life breathed into him by God (Gen. 2:7), a woman was the first to see him, for Eve was the first human being after him. In the same way, no one saw the second Adam, that is the Lord, rising from the dead, since none of his disciples were present and the soldiers keeping the tomb had been shaken with fear and became like dead men. But after the Resurrection it was a woman who saw Him first of all, as we heard today in Mark's Gospel. "Now when Jesus", it says, "was risen early the first day of the week, he appeared first to Mary Magdalene" (Mark 16:9).

The Evangelist seems to be telling us clearly that it was early morning when the Lord rose, that He appeared first to Mary Magdalene, and that He appeared at the very time of the Resurrection. However, this is not what he says, as will become clear if we look more carefully. A little earlier Mark, together with the other Evangelists, says that this Mary had also come earlier to the tomb with the other myrrhbearers, and finding it empty, they went away (Mark 16:1–8). So the Lord had risen long before that hour of the morning when she saw Him. When the Evangelist indicates the time of that earlier visit, he does not say simply "early", as he does here, but "very early in the morning". There they called the first hint of pale light on the horizon sunrise, as John shows by saying that Mary Magdalene came "early, when it was yet dark, unto the sepulchre, and seeth the stone taken away from the sepulchre" (John 20:1).

According to John, she did not just come to the sepulchre at that time, but left it without seeing the Lord. She ran and came to Peter and John and told them, not that the Lord had risen, but that He had been taken from the sepulchre, as she was not yet aware of the Resurrection (John 20:2). So the Lord did not appear to Mary absolutely first of all, but when full daylight had come. There is something which the Evangelists tell us in a veiled way, but which I shall reveal to your charity. As was right and just, the Mother of God was the first person to receive from the Lord the Good News of the Resurrection, and she saw Him risen and had the joy of His divine words before anyone else. She not only beheld Him with her eyes and heard Him with her ears, but was the first and only person to touch with her hands His most pure feet. If the Evangelists do not say all this openly it is because they do not want to put forward His Mother as a witness, lest they give unbelievers grounds for suspicion. As we are now, however, by the grace of the Resurrection, addressing believers, and the subject of today's feast obliges us to clarify everything that concerns the myrrhbearers, this too shall be revealed, with leave from Him Who said, "Nothing is secret, that shall not be made manifest" (Luke 8:17).

The myrrhbearers are those women who followed the Lord in company with His Mother, who stayed with her at the time of the saving Passion, and were intent upon anointing the Lord's Body with myrrh. When Joseph and Nicodemus sought and obtained the Master's Body from Pilate, they took it down from the Cross, wrapped it in linen cloths with glue-like spices, put it in a sepulchre hewn out of a rock and put a large stone in the doorway (John 19:38–42). Meanwhile, according to the Evangelist Mark, Mary Magdalene and the other Mary were there watching (Mark 15:47), sitting opposite the tomb. When he refers to the other Mary he clearly means the Mother of God, for she was also called the mother of Joses and James, the sons of Joseph the Betrothed. But they were not the only ones there watching when the Lord was being laid in the tomb. There were other women as well, as Luke tells us when he writes, "And the women also, which came with him from Galilee, followed after, and beheld the sepulchre, and how his body was laid" (Luke 23:55). "It was Mary Magdalene and Joanna and Mary the Mother of James and other women that were with them" (Luke 24:10).

He says that they returned and bought spices and ointments (cf. Luke 23:56). As yet they did not fully understand that He Himself is truly the fragrance of life for those who come to Him in faith, though the smell of death to those who are disobedient to the end. The scent of His garments, that is of His body, is above all spices, and His "name is like ointment poured forth" (Song of Songs 1:3), filling the whole world with divine fragrance. They prepared myrrh and spices, intending, on the one hand, to honour the dead, and, on the other, to assuage by their anointing the stench of the body as it decomposed, for the sake of those who wanted to stay beside it.

When they had prepared the ointments and spices, they rested on the Sabbath according to the commandment (Luke 23:56), for they had not yet understood the true Sabbaths, nor had they discovered that exceedingly blessed Sabbath which brought human nature up from the nethermost regions of Hades to divine, heavenly heights full of light. "Now upon the first day of the week, at early dawn", as Luke tells us, "they came unto the sepulchre, bringing the spices which they had prepared" (cf. Luke 24:1). However, Matthew says that it was "In the end of the sabbath, as it began to dawn toward the first day of the week" (Matt. 28:1), and refers to two women coming. According to John, "it was yet dark" (John 20:1), and only Mary Magdalene approached, whereas Mark tells us it was, "very early in the morning the first day of the week" (Mark 16:2), and there were three women who came (Mark 16:1). The Evangelists all call Sunday the first day of the week, and by the expressions, "the end of the sabbath", "at the early dawn", "very early in the morning", and "early, when it was yet dark", they mean the time around dawn when light and darkness mingle. This is when the eastern horizon begins to grow light, heralding the day. If you were to observe the horizon from afar, you might see it beginning to be tinged with light at about the ninth hour of the night, with three hours still to go before full daylight.

The Evangelists seem to a certain extent to disagree about what time it was and how many women were there. This is because, as we have said, there were many myrrhbearers and they did not come just once to the tomb, but two or three times. They came in groups, but not always the same women. They all came at dawn, but not at precisely the same time, and Mary Magdalene came once more on her own and stayed longer. Each Evangelist refers to one of the occasions when the myrrhbearers approached, and passes over the others. However, I conclude and infer from all the Evangelists, as I said before, that the Theotokos was the first to come to the tomb of her Son and God, bringing Mary Magdalene with her. I gather this above all from the Evangelist Matthew who says, "There came Mary Magdalene and the other Mary", who was obviously the Mother of God, "to see the sepulchre. And, behold, there was a great earthquake: for the angel of the Lord descended from heaven, and came and rolled back the stone from the door of the sepulchre, and sat upon it. His countenance was like lightning, and his raiment white as snow: and for fear of him the keepers did shake, and became as dead men" (Matt. 28:1–4).

All the other women came after the earthquake when the keepers had fled, and found the sepulchre open and the stone rolled away. The Virgin Mother, however, was there when the earthquake took place, the stone was rolled away, the tomb opened and the keepers were still present, though shaken with fear. When they got to their feet after the earthquake they immediately took to flight, whereas the Mother of God delighted herself in the sight without fear. It seems to me that the life-bearing tomb opened first for her sake (because everything in heaven above and on earth below was opened first for her, and through her for us) and that the angel shone like lightning on her account, so that even though it was still dark, by the angel's abundant light she could see not only the empty tomb, but also the graveclothes lying in order and bearing witness in many ways to the fact that He Who had been buried there had risen.

The Angel who announced the Good News was surely Gabriel himself. For when he who had originally said to her, "Fear not, Mary: for thou hast found favour with God" (Luke 1:30), saw her hastening to the tomb, he made speed now to come down and greet the Ever-Virgin once more with the same words, to announce the Good News that He Who had been born of her without seed had risen from the dead, to take away the stone, and to show the empty tomb and the graveclothes as confirmation to her of his tidings. "And the angel", it says, "answered and said unto the women, Fear not ye: do ye seek Jesus, which was crucified? He is risen. Come, see the place where the Lord lay" (Matt. 28:5–6). "Even though", he says, "you see the keepers struck down with fear, you are not to be afraid. I know that you seek Jesus Who was crucified. He is risen, He is not here. Not only can He not be held by the locks, bars and seals of Hades, death and the tomb, but He is also Lord of us, the immortal, heavenly angels, and He alone is Lord of all." "Come, see", he says, "the place where the Lord lay. And go quickly, and tell his disciples that he is risen from the dead" (Matt. 28:6–7).

"And they departed", it says, "with fear and great joy" (Matt. 28:8). Once more it seems to me that it was Mary Magdalene and the other women who had gathered with them by this time who still felt fear. For they had not understood the force of the angel's words, nor could they fully perceive the light so as to see and discover exactly what had happened. It was the Mother of God, on the other hand, who was possessed of great joy, because she understood what the angel said and was completely filled with light, being utterly purified and full of divine grace. Therefore she knew the truth for sure and believed the Archangel, since his trustworthiness had long since been demonstrated to her through works. As the divinely wise Virgin was present when these things happened, how could she fail to understand what had been accomplished? She saw an earthquake, and a great one at that, an angel descending from heaven, flashing forth as lightning, she saw the keepers being struck down as dead, and the stone being moved, and the tomb empty. She also saw the great miracle of the graveclothes, which had not been undone and were held together with myrrh and aloes, but were visibly empty of the Body. In addition to all this, there was the angel's joyful appearance and message to her. But when they had departed after these good tidings, it was as if Mary Magdalene had not heard the Angel, or perhaps his greeting was not for her, since her only precise statement was that the sepulchre was empty, and she made no mention of the graveclothes. "Then she runneth, and cometh to Simon Peter, and to the other disciple", as John tells us (John 20:2).

The Virgin Mother of God, on the other hand, returned in the company of other women to the place whence she had come. And behold, as Matthew says, "Jesus met them, saying, All hail". Notice that the Mother of God saw Him Who for our salvation suffered in the flesh, was buried and rose again, even before Mary Magdalene. "And they came", it says, "and held him by the feet and worshipped him" (Matt. 28:9). When the Theotokos, together with Mary Magdalene, heard the Good News of the Resurrection from the Angel, only she understood the meaning of the words. In the same way now when, in the company of the other women, she met her Son and God, she was the first of them all to see and recognize the risen Lord, and falling down before Him she grasped His feet and became His Apostle to the Apostles. It is from John that we learn that Mary Magdalene was not with the Mother of God at the time when the Lord met her as she was returning from the tomb, appeared to her and addressed her. For John says that Mary Magdalene "runneth, and cometh to Simon

Peter, and to the other disciple, whom Jesus loved, and saith unto them, They have taken away the Lord out of the sepulchre, and we know not where they have laid him" (John 20:2). If He had met her and she had seen Him, touched Him with her hands and heard Him speak, how could she have said, as she did, that they had taken Him away and laid Him in an unknown place? But after Peter and John had run to the tomb and seen the linen cloths, and gone away, "Mary", it says, "stood without at the sepulchre weeping" (John 20:11).

Observe that not only had she yet to hear Him, but she also had yet to hear the news. When the angels appeared and asked her, "Woman, why weepest thou", again, she replied as if speaking about a corpse (John 20:13). Even when she turned round and saw the Lord, she still did not understand, but when He too asked why she was weeping she gave the same reply, until He called her by name and proved it was He. Then she too fell down before Him and tried to embrace His feet in greeting, but heard Him say, "Touch me not" (John 20:15-17). From this we learn that when the Lord appeared earlier to His Mother and the women with her, it was only His Mother whom He allowed to touch His feet, even though Matthew attributes this action to the other women too, being unwilling to put forward the Lord's Mother as a witness to such events for the reason we stated in the beginning.

The Ever-Virgin was the first to come to the tomb and receive the good tidings of the Resurrection, but afterwards many women came together and they too saw the stone rolled away and heard the angels. Then after seeing and hearing, they separated. Some, as Mark tells us, "fled from the sepulchre, for they trembled and were amazed: neither said they any thing to any man, for they were afraid" (Mark 16:8). Others followed the Lord's Mother, and these it was who had the good fortune to see the Master and be addressed by Him. Mary Magdalene, on the other hand, went to tell Peter and John, and returned with them to the tomb on her own. When they left she stayed, and she too was accounted worthy to see the Master, and was sent to the Apostles. Once more she came to them to tell them all, as John says, "that she had seen the

Lord, and that he had spoken these things unto her" (John 20:18). Mark tells us that the Lord appeared to Mary Magdalene early in the morning (*cf.* Mark 16:9), which means when full daylight had come, obviously after dawn had passed, but he does not state that the Lord's Resurrection happened then or that it was the first time He had appeared.

So now we have a thorough explanation of everything that concerns the myrrhbearers, and, as we have sought all along, agreement between the four Evangelists on this subject. On the very day of the Resurrection the Apostles heard from the myrrhbearers, from Peter (Luke 24:34), and from Luke and Cleopas (Mark 16:12–13; *cf.* Luke 24:13–35), that the Lord was alive and had appeared to them, but they did not believe. That is why they were reproached by Him when He appeared to them later when they were gathered together (Mark 16:14). However, once He had shown Himself in many ways and on many occasions to be alive, not only did they all believe, but they preached everywhere: "Their sound is gone out through all the earth, and their words to the end of the world" (Ps. 19:6 Lxx; Rom. 10:18), "The Lord working with them, and confirming the word with signs following" (Mark 16:20). For signs were absolutely necessary until the word had been preached throughout the world. But if there had to be great signs to prove and confirm that the teaching was true, there had also to be signs, though not great ones, to show whether those who had received the word really believed. What signs do I mean? The witness of their deeds. "Show me", it says, "thy faith by thy works" (*cf.* Jas. 2:18), and, "Who is faithful? By his good life let him show his works" (*cf.* Jas. 3:13). How can we believe that someone has a truly divine, great, exalted, even heavenly understanding, such as godliness entails, if he clings to sordid actions and is engrossed in the earth and its concerns?

It is pointless for someone to say that he has faith in God if he does not have the works which go with faith. What benefit were their lamps to the foolish virgins who had no oil (Matt. 25:1–13), namely, deeds of love and compassion? What good did calling Abraham his father do to that rich man frying in the unquenchable flame for his pitilessness towards Lazarus (Luke 16:19–31)? What use was his apparent obedience to the invitation to that man who had failed to acquire through good works a garment fitting for the divine wedding and the bridechamber of immortality? He was invited and approached because he clearly believed, and he sat down alongside those holy guests, but when he was convicted and put to shame for being clothed in depraved habits and deeds, he was mercilessly bound hand and foot, and cast into hellfire, where there is weeping and gnashing of teeth (Matt. 22:11–14).

May no one called by Christ have this experience, but may we all display a way of life which goes with our faith, that we may enter the bridechamber of unfading joy and spend eternity with the saints in the dwelling place of all those who rejoice. Amen.

ON THE DORMITION

BOTH LONGING AND OBLIGATION compose my homily today to your charity. It is not just my desire out of love for you and my duty under sacred laws to fill your pious ears with saving words to nourish your souls, but there is also nothing dearer or more necessary for me than to expound with due honour in church the wonders of the ever-virgin Mother of God. This longing, not single but twofold, persuades, beseeches, and encourages me, whereas inescapable duty compels me. Words, however, cannot attain to what is beyond speech, just as eyes cannot stare at the sun. But though it is impossible for us to tell of things surpassing words, we can, by the love of those we extol, sing their praises, and we may use words to pay our debt, and express our longing for the Mother of God in hymns as best we can, without in any way touching the intangible.

If "precious in the sight of the Lord is the death of his saints" (Ps. 116:15), and "the memory of the just is praised" (Prov. 10:7 Lxx), how much more fitting is it for us to celebrate with highest honours the memory of the ever-virgin Mother of God, the Holy of Holies, through whom the saints receive their hallowing? That is exactly what we are doing today by commemorating her holy dormition and passing away, through which, having been made a little lower than the angels (*cf.* Ps. 8:5), she rose incomparably higher than the Angels, Archangels, and all the heavenly powers above them, because of her nearness to the God of all (cf. Rom. 9:5), and the marvels written of old which were accomplished in her.

On her account there were divine predictions by prophets inspired by God. Miracles foreshadowed the great future wonder of the world, the Ever-virgin Mother of God. Nations and circumstances were transformed to make way for the fulfilment of the new mystery concerning her. Spiritual ordinances prefigured in all sorts of ways the truth that was to be. The culmination, or rather the beginning and foundation of subsequent marvellous events, was the accomplishment of God's promise to Joachim and Anna, the most virtuous people of their day, that, although childless from their youth, they would have a child in their extreme old age, and that their daughter would bear without seed Him Whom God the Father had begotten before all ages, outside time. In addition, those who were to become parents in this mysterious way vowed to give back the child, who was to give birth herself even more mysteriously, to the Giver of the gift. In accordance with this worthiest of vows, the Mother of God left her father's house in extraordinary fashion while still an infant, to live in God's house. For the space of many years she stayed there, strange as it seems, in the Holy of Holies, provided with indescribable nourishment by attending angels: food, which Adam never reached the point of tasting, otherwise he would not have fallen away from life; as was the case with the all-pure Virgin, who now passes from earth to heaven – even though for Adam's sake and to show herself his daughter, she, like her Son, yielded for a short time to nature.

After this unutterable nourishment came the mysterious divine plan for the Virgin's betrothal, the strange, inexplicable greeting of the Archangel who flew down from on high, and God's messages and salutations, which reversed Adam and Eve's condemnation, and healed the curse which was upon them, turning it into a blessing (Luke 1:28–38). For the King of all desired the secret beauty of the Ever-Virgin, as David foretold (cf. Ps. 45:11). He bowed the heavens and came down (Ps. 18:9), and overshadowed her (cf. Luke 1:35), rather, the power of the

Most High came to dwell in her in His very person. He did not reveal His presence through darkness and fire, as He did to Moses (*cf.* Exod. 19:16, 18), nor through a tempest and cloud, as He did to Elijah (*cf.* 1 Kgs. 18:45), but the unveiled power of the Most High directly overshadowed the Virgin's perfectly pure womb with nothing intervening, neither the air of earth or heaven, nor anything visible or invisible. For this was not overshadowing, but pure union.

Since anything that overshadows something else naturally gives it its own form and character, what came to pass in the Virgin's womb was not just union but the formation, out of both the power of the Most High and her all-holy virgin womb, of the incarnate Word of God. The Word of God in the flesh made His abode in her, came forth from her, "and appeared on earth and went about among men". He made our human nature divine, and bestowed on us, according to the holy Apostle, "things the angels desire to look into" (1 Pet. 1:12). Such is the extraordinary honour and all-surpassing glory of the Ever-Virgin, which defeats the mind and speech of all, however angelic they be. Again, what words can express the events that followed this indescribable Birth? Co-operating with, and sharing in the sufferings of, the self-emptying of the Word of God (*cf.* Phil. 2:7), which was accomplished through her, and led to His exaltation, she was justly glorified and lifted up with Him, constantly adding great gifts to the extraordinary ones already bestowed upon her. Even after He Who took flesh from her ascended into heaven, it was as though she was striving to emulate the great works past understanding and speech which He had wrought in her, through patient endurance in all kinds of asceticism, through prayers and exertions for the whole world, and counsels and exhortations for those going to the ends of the earth to preach. She was the sole support and consolation of all who saw or heard her, assisting by various means in the proclamation of the Gospel. Thus she showed that her whole life, her behaviour, her mind and her words, were utterly devoted to godly striving.

As a result of this, her death, too, was life-giving and led to heavenly, immortal life, and its day of remembrance is a joyful holiday and worldwide festival. Not only does it renew the memory of the wonders of the Mother of God, it also commemorates the unheard-of way in which all the holy Apostles were gathered from every country to her sacred funeral, the hymns of divine revelation sung on that occasion by these inspired men, the attendance of angels, singing and ministering around her. They escorted her and followed behind, they aided or opposed, protected and defended, and with all their might assisted in deed and song, those who in any way reverenced that body which had held God and is the starting-point of life, the saving remedy of our human race, solemnly chosen from the whole Creation. On the other hand, they secretly fought and opposed the Jews when they insulted her and rebelled against God in thought and deed. The Lord of Hosts, meanwhile, the Son of the Ever-Virgin, was invisibly present, honouring His Mother's departure. Into His hands she entrusted her God-bearing spirit, and through Him her body, her spirit's companion, was soon translated into a heavenly place of eternal life, as rightly befits her whole life from the very beginning.

In ancient times there were many who attained to divine favour, glory, and power. As David says, "How precious also are thy friends unto me, O God! How great is their authority! If I should count them, they are more in number than the sand" (Ps. 139:17–18 Lxx). According to Solomon, "Many have acquired riches, and many daughters have acted with power, but she excels and outdoes them all", to an inexpressible degree (cf. Prov. 31:29). Standing between God and the whole human race, she alone made God a son of man, and men sons of God, rendered the earth heaven and made mankind divine. She alone among women was declared the Mother of God by nature transcending every nature. Through her unutterable childbearing she became Queen of all Creation in this world and beyond, and through herself she raised up those below her, and made her subjects heavenly instead of earthly. She shared in the noblest honour, the most sublime power and the ordination bestowed from heaven through the divine Spirit (*cf.* Acts 1:14; 2:1–4), and was set high above all, the supremely blessed Queen of a blessed race.

Today she has moved from earth to heaven, and now has heaven too as a fitting dwelling-place, a palace meet for her. She has stood on the right hand of the King of all, clothed in vesture wrought with gold, and arrayed in divers colours, as the Psalmist and Prophet says of her (*cf.* Ps. 45:9 Lxx); and you should take this garment interwoven with gold to mean her divinely radiant body, adorned with every type of virtue. For at present she is the only one who has a place in heaven with her divinely glorified body in the company of her Son. Earth, the grave and death could not ultimately detain her life-giving body, which has held God and been a more beloved habitation for Him than heaven and the heaven of heavens. For if a soul which has the grace of God dwelling within it goes up to heaven when released from this world, as we believe and is evident on many accounts, how can that body which not only received within it the pre-eternal, only-begotten Son of God, the ever-flowing Fount of grace, but was also plainly seen to bear Him, fail to be taken up from earth to heaven? Could she who, when only three years old, before the heavenly Child had dwelt within her and been clothed by her in flesh, lived in the Holy of Holies, and who became excellent and truly heavenly even in her body through many great works, afterwards become earth subject to corruption? How could this seem reasonable to people who take a rational view?

It was right, therefore, that the body which brought forth the Son should be glorified with Him in divine glory, and that the Ark of Christ's holiness should arise with Him Who rose on the third day, as the Prophet sang (*cf.* Ps. 132:8 Lxx). The linen cloths and winding-sheets left behind in the tomb, which were all that those who came to look for her found there, proved to the disciples that she too had risen from the dead, just as was earlier the case with her Son and Lord (*cf.* Luke 24:12; John 20:5–7). It was not, however, necessary for her, as it was for her Son and God, to stay for a while longer on earth, so she was taken up directly from the grave to the heavenly realm, whence she sends bright shafts of holy light and grace down to earth, illuminating all the space around the world, and is venerated, admired, and hymned by all the faithful.

It is as though God wanted to set up an icon of everything good and, in so doing, to display His own image clearly to angels and men, and thus He made her so truly beautiful. Bringing together all the various means He had used to adorn all Creation, He made her a world of everything good, both visible and invisible. Or rather, He revealed her as the synthesis of divine, angelic and human loveliness, a nobler beauty to embellish both worlds, originating from the earth but reaching up, through her ascension now from the tomb to heaven, to the heavens and beyond. She united things below with things above, and embraces the whole of Creation with the wonders surrounding her. The fact that she tasted death, which, as I mentioned in the beginning, meant she was a little lower than the angels, increases the universal excellence of the Mother of God. That is why all things rightly join together to rejoice at the celebration today of this event.

It is fitting that she, who held Him Who fills all things and is above all things, should herself outstrip all, and become higher than all in her virtues and great honour. She embraces in their entirety the virtues which, distributed among the noblest of every age, were sufficient to make them great, and the various graces with which angels and men have individually been favoured by God, and perfects them all in herself alone with inexpressible excellence. Also, she is superior to everyone in that after death she became immortal, and she alone lives in her body with her Son and God in heaven. Thence she pours down abundant grace on those who honour her and bestows on them the possibility of reaching up to her, the receptacle of such great graces, who lavishes the highest benefits upon us in her goodness, and never ceases to yield a rich harvest and plentiful gifts for us. Anyone observing her help and generosity in everything good would say that, for those who live virtuously, the Virgin radiates virtue as the sun radiates visible light for those dwelling below. But were you to shift your mental gaze to the Sun Who marvellously shone forth to mankind from her, and Who possesses by His very nature everything bestowed on her by grace, and far more besides, then the Virgin would immediately seem like heaven to you. Having a far more abundant share in God's good things than all other recipients of His grace in heaven or below, she is as much greater than them as the heavens are greater than the sun, though the Sun is brighter.

What words can describe your divinely-radiant beauty, O Virgin Mother of God? We cannot circumscribe you in our words and thoughts, for everything about you surpasses our speech and understanding. But, with your loving permission, we may sing your praises. In you all graces find a place. You are the fullness of everything noble and good, a living picture and icon of all goodness and kindness, for you alone were found worthy of the gifts of the Spirit in their entirety, or rather, you alone had mysteriously dwelling in your womb Him in Whom all these gifts were stored. In a way past understanding, you became His Tabernacle, and now through death you proceed hence to immortality, and are fittingly translated from earth to heaven, to live with Him for ever in the heavenly tabernacles. From there you care for your inheritance, and by your unsleeping intercessions you reconcile us to your Son.

The Mother of God is so much closer to God than others who draw near to Him that she is able to intercede more powerfully than any of them, and by this I mean not just human beings but even all the ranks of angels. Isaiah writes of the highest order of angels in heaven, "And the Seraphim stood round about Him" (Isa. 6:2 Lxx), whereas David says of the Mother of God, "Upon thy right hand did stand the queen" (Ps. 45:9). Do you notice the difference in their standing? You can also see from this the difference in honour between the Seraphim's rank and hers, for the Seraphim are "round about" God, but only the Queen of all stands beside Him. She is admired and praised by God Himself, as though He were extolling her to the powers around Him in the words used in the Song of Songs, "How beautiful is my companion!" (*cf.* Song of Songs 4:1; 6:4 Lxx). She is more brilliant than light, she blossoms more beautifully than the gardens of divine paradise, and she is more delightfully adorned

than the visible and invisible worlds. It is fitting that she stands
not just beside God, but on His right hand, for where Christ sat in
heaven, namely, on the right hand of the majesty (Heb. 1:3), there
she now stands, having ascended from earth to heaven. Nor is this
solely because no one longs for Christ as she does, and no one is so
longed for in return, which would be in accordance with the laws
of nature, but because she is truly His throne; and where the King
sits, there stands the throne.

Isaiah saw this throne in the midst of the choir of Cherubim,
and described it as "high and lifted up" (Isa. 6:1), thus indicating
that the Mother of God had risen higher than the heavenly powers.
For that reason he refers to the angels themselves glorifying God
for her and saying, "Blessed be the glory of the Lord from his
place" (Ezek. 3:12). The Patriarch Jacob, seeing obscure glimpses
of this throne, said, "How dreadful is this place! This is none other
but the house of God, and this is the gate of heaven" (Gen. 28:17).
Elsewhere, David, uniting in himself all the multitude of the saved,
and using as different strings or notes all those brought together
from diverse races into one faith by the Ever-Virgin, plays a most
harmonious song to her, with the words, "I will make thy name
to be remembered in all generations: therefore shall the people
praise thee for ever, even for ever and ever" (Ps. 45:17).

Notice how all Creation praises the Virgin Mother, not just in
past times, but "for ever, even for ever and ever". From this we can
see that she will never cease doing good to the whole of Creation,
not just to the human race, but also to the immaterial supernatural
hosts of angels. The fact that they, like us, partake of and touch
the intangible divine nature only through her is clearly shown
by Isaiah. For he did not see the Seraphim taking the live coal
directly off the altar, but picking it up with tongs, which he also
used to touch his prophetic lips to purify them (Isa. 6:6–7). This
vision of the tongs is the same as that great vision which Moses
saw of the bush burning with fire but not consumed (Exod. 3:2).
Is there anyone who is unaware that the Virgin Mother is both
that bush and those tongs, which held the divine fire without
being burnt; for was it not to this very mystery that the Archangel

ministered at her conception, which united through her the One Who takes away the sin of the world with the race of men, and which, through this indescribable union, has thoroughly cleansed us? She alone stands at the border between created and uncreated nature, and no one can come to God unless he is truly illumined by her, the true lamp of divine radiance. "For God is in the midst of her", says the Scripture, "she shall not be moved" (Ps. 46:5).

God requites us according to the measure of our love for Him, and he who loves the Son is loved by Him and by His Father, and becomes a place for them both to dwell, secretly living within him and going about with him, as the Lord promised (cf. John 4:21–23). But who could love the Son more than His Mother, who did not just bear Him as her only child, but gave birth alone to Him without a husband, such that her parental love was twice as strong, since it was not shared with a spouse? Or who could be more loved by the only-begotten Son than His Mother, especially as He came forth ineffably from her alone in the last times, as He had come forth from the Father alone before time began? How could He Who came down to fulfil the Law (cf. Matt. 5:17) fail to increase many times over, in addition to the loving disposition expected of a son, the honour due to His Mother under that Law?

Just as it was only through her that the Son came to us, was seen on earth, and lived among men, after previously being invisible to all, so from now on for endless eternity all progress towards the manifestation of divine light, every revelation of divine mysteries, and all forms of spiritual gifts are beyond everyone's grasp without her. She was the first to receive the all-pervading fullness of Him Who fills all things (Eph. 1:23; cf. 4:10), and she brought Him within reach of all, distributing to each as he is able to receive, in proportion to the measure of his purity, such that she is both the treasure-house and Mistress of God's riches.

It is an eternal custom in heaven that those who are lesser should participate through those who are greater in what lies beyond existence, and the Virgin Mother is incomparably greater than all. So as many as will share in God will do so through her, all those who know God will know her as the one who holds Him

Whom nothing can contain, and all who sing God's praises will hymn her after God. She is the cause of what preceded her, the protectress of what comes after her, and she procures eternity. She is the prophets' theme, the Apostles' starting point, the martyrs' mainstay, and the teachers' foundation. Of all those on earth she is the glory, of those in heaven the delight, the adornment of all Creation. Source, fount and root of ineffable good things, she is the crown and perfection of all the saints.

O holy and now heavenly Virgin, how can I fully describe you? How can I glorify the treasure-house of glory? Just the remembrance of you brings hallowing. Simply turning towards you makes our mind more lucid, and takes it straight up to divine heights. Through you the eye of our understanding is sharpened; through you our spirit is enlightened by the Coming of the divine Spirit. You have become the treasurer of graces and their store, not so you might keep them for yourself, but that you might fill the universe with grace. For the trustee of inexhaustible treasures sees to their distribution. Why would never-dwindling wealth be locked away?

Therefore, O Lady, generously share your mercy and your graces with all your people, your inheritance. Rescue us from the terrors that encompass us. See how many dangers of all kinds afflict us, from our own people and from strangers, from within and without. Through your power turn everything for the best. Bring mutual calm between fellow-citizens at home, and drive away those who attack like wild beasts from outside. Bestow your aid and healing on us to counteract our passions, and give our souls and bodies abundant grace sufficient for every need. And if we are unable to contain it, increase our capacity and give us more, that saved and strengthened by your grace we may glorify the pre-eternal Word, Who took flesh from you for our sake, together with His Father without beginning and the life-giving Spirit, now and for ever and unto unending ages. Amen.